JAPAN YESTERDAY AND TODAY

THE GEORGE SCHOOL READINGS ON DEVELOPING LANDS

Series Editors: Clark D. Moore and David W. Miller

Japan Yesterday and Today

EDITED BY

RAY F. DOWNS

PRAEGER PUBLISHERS
New York · Washington · London

PRAEGER PUBLISHERS
111 Fourth Avenue, New York, N.Y. 10003, U.S.A.
5, Cromwell Place, London S.W.7, England

Published in the United States of America in 1970
by Praeger Publishers, Inc.

Library of Congress Catalog Card Number: 79–83341

Printed in the United States of America

Acknowledgments

The United States and Japan *by Edwin O. Reischauer. Harvard University Press. Copyright 1950, 1957, and 1965 by the President and Fellows of Harvard University and reprinted with their permission.*

Ancient Japan *by J. Edward Kidder. The John Day Co., Inc. Reprinted by permission of the John Day Company and Weidenfield & Nicolson, Ltd.*

Living Japan *by Donald Keene. Published in 1959 by Doubleday & Co., Inc. A Chanticleer Press Edition.*

Nihongi: Chronicles of Japan from Earliest Times A. D. 670 *translated by W. G. Aston. George Allen & Unwin, Ltd; reprinted with their permission.*

"The Season of Instant Worshippers" by Shukan Bunshun. THE JAPAN TIMES; *January 3, 1969; reprinted with their permission.*

The Enduring Art of Japan *by Langdon Warner. Harvard University Press. Copyright 1952 by the President and Fellows of Harvard College and reprinted with their permission.*

Twelve Doors to Japan *by J. W. Hall and R. K. Beardsley. McGraw-Hill Book Company. Copyright © 1965 by McGraw-Hill Book Company and reprinted with their permission.*

The World of the Shining Prince *by Ivan Morris. Alfred A. Knopf, Inc. Copyright © 1964 by Ivan Morris. Reprinted by permission of Alfred A. Knopf, Inc., Oxford University Press, Ltd., and Julian Bach Associates.*

Japanese Literature: An Introduction for Western Readers *by Donald Keene. John Murray, Ltd.; reprinted with their permission.*

East Asia: The Great Tradition *by Edwin O. Reischauer and J. K. Fairbank. Houghton Mifflin Company. Reprinted with permission of the publishers.*

Sources of Japanese Tradition *edited by Tsunoda, DeBary, and Keene. Columbia University Press; Copyright © 1958 by Columbia University Press and reprinted with their permission.*

Anthology of Japanese Literature *by Donald Keene. G. W. Sargent, translator. Grove Press. Reprinted by permission of G. W. Sargent.*

Bushido: The Soul of Japan *by Inazo Nitobe. G. P. Putnam & Sons; copyright 1905 by Putnam's & Coward McCann and reprinted with their permission.*

East Asia: The Modern Transformation *by J. K. Fairbank, Edwin O. Reischauer and A. M. Craig. Reprinted with permission of the publisher, Houghton Mifflin Company.*

A History of Modern Japan *by R. Storry. Reprinted with permission of the publisher, Penguin Books, Ltd.*

Modern Japanese Literature: An Anthology *edited by Donald Keene. Grove Press. Copyright © 1956 by Grove Press and reprinted with the permission of Grove Press and Thames & Hudson, Ltd.*

Japanese Government Documents: Transactions of the Asiatic Society of Japan. *Edited by W. W. McLaren. Asiatic Society of Japan.*

Commentaries on the Constitution of the Empire of Japan *by Ito Herobumi; translated by Ito Myoji. Nippon Chosakuken Kyogikai.*

The Japan Yearbook 1939–1940 *in Modern Japan; Anvil #9 by Arthur Tiedemann. D. Van Nostrand Co., Inc. Copyright 1955 by Arthur Tiedemann and reprinted with the permission of Van Nostrand Reinhold Co.*

The United States and Japan *edited by H. Passin. Prentice-Hall, Inc. Copyright © 1966 by The American Assembly, Columbia University. Reprinted by permission of Prentice-Hall, Inc.*

Unwilling Patriot *by T. Aikawa, Jordan Press, Tokyo.*

Hiroshima Diary *by Michihiko Hachiya. Translated by Dr. Warner Wells. Reprinted with the permission of the publishers, University of North Carolina Press.*

Facts About Japan, Number 81. *Consulate General of Japan. Reprinted with the permission of the Consulate General of Japan.*

"Japan Tries for a Second Miracle" *by Peter Drucker in* HARPER'S MAGAZINE, *March, 1963. Copyright © 1963 by Harper's Magazine, Inc. Reprinted by permission of the author.*

Beyond Vietnam *by E. O. Reischauer. Alfred A. Knopf, Inc. Copyright © 1967 by Edwin O. Reischauer. Reprinted by permission of Alfred A. Knopf, Inc. and Oxford University Press.*

"A Japanese View of America" *by Masatuka Kosaka in* HARPER'S MAGAZINE, *May 1965. Copyright © 1965 by Harper's Magazine Inc.; reprinted by permission of the author.*

"Resetting the Course" *by Shintaro Ryu.* JAPAN QUARTERLY. *Reprinted with the permission of* JAPAN QUARTERLY.

"Traditional Arts and the Japanese Sense of Historical Identity During a Hundred Years of Modern Change" *by John W. Hall in* BULLETIN ON JAPANESE CULTURE #91. *Copyright © 1968 by Kokusai Bunka Shinkokai, Tokyo. Reprinted by permission of the author.*

CONTENTS

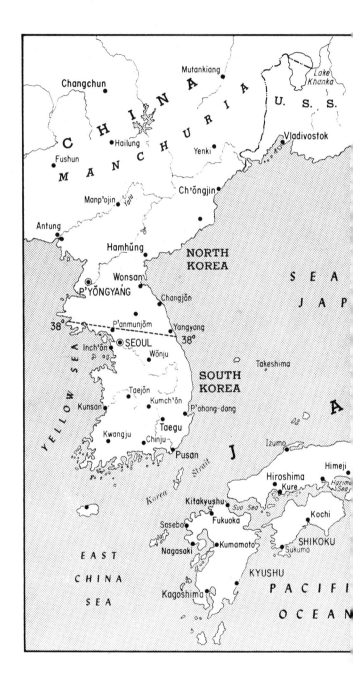

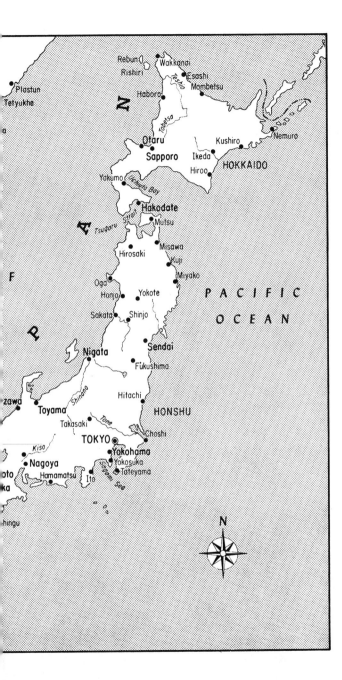

CHRONOLOGY

It is wise to approach any time line or chronology with caution. The sophisticated observer will want to know what criteria have been used in identifying "major events" and demarcating periods. A periodization appropriate to the political history of a nation may not be logical for studying economic, social, or artistic development. The following chronology follows the mode made popular by Japanese political historians of the nineteenth century. The basic criteria for demarcation (excluding prehistoric and modern times) are the shifts in the location of the "power center" and in the family holding power.

Prehistoric Period (before c. 300 A.D.)

"Prepottery" Culture (20,000? B.C.–c. 4500 B.C.)

A paleolithic culture whose existence has only been confirmed in recent years.

Jomon Culture (c. 4500–250 B.C.)

A "mesolithic" culture dependent upon hunting, fishing, and gathering. Distinctive pottery. Village sites scattered over most of Japan.

Yayoi Culture (c. 250 B.C.–300 A.D.)

Neolithic culture. Introduction of rice agriculture and bronze casting. Probable evolution of Japanese language and Shinto religion. Perhaps the first "Japanese" culture.

Yamato Period (c. 300–710)

The "semihistoric" tomb culture provides the context for the rise of many "clans" ruled by warrior artistocrats claiming religious sanctions. The Yamato "clan" gradually gains control over western Japan and constitutes a "government" by the early fifth century. Rapid importation of Chinese culture begins after 587.

Nara Period (710–794)

First permanent capital built on Chinese plan at Nara. Further growth of Buddhism and Chinese-style bureaucratic government.

Heian (Fujiwara) Period (794–1185)

New capital at Heian (Kyoto). Growth of native culture as Chinese influence wanes. Fujiwara family controls a simplified government as emperors become figureheads.

Kamakura Period (1185–1333)

The first stage in the evolution of feudalism as a warrior class loyal to the shoguns ("generalissimo") at Kamakura (near Tokyo) controls the country. Popularization of Buddhism. Mongol invasions thwarted.

Muromachi (Ashikaga) Period (1333–1568)

Second stage of feudalism as the Ashikaga *shoguns* lose power to the rising daimyos (feudal lords) ruling independent *hans* (domains). Active commerce and foreign trade. Flourishing of Zen-inspired arts. Western missionaries and traders arrive in mid-sixteenth century.

Azuchi-Momoyama Period (1568–1600)

> Unification by Hideyoshi and others as daimyos become subject to central authority. Unsuccessful invasion of Korea.

Tokugawa (Edo) Period (1600–1868)

> Strong centralized authority over daimyos maintained by "military bureaucracy." Tokugawa headquarters in Edo (Tokyo). Self-imposed isolation from 1639 to 1853. Substantial urban growth and rise of merchant culture.

Modern Period (1868–   )
Meiji Period (1868–1912)

> Vigorous modernization as Japan becomes a world power. Taiwan and Korea added to the empire after successful wars with China and Russia. Foundation of parliamentary system laid.

Taisho (1912–1926) and Showa (1926–   ) Periods

> Liberalism of 1920s followed by totalitarian trends and defeat in World War II. Japan reaches new heights of prosperity under democratic government following seven-year occupation.

PART I. THE FOUNDATIONS

The Impact of Geography on Japanese Culture

"One hundred million people in an area the size of California!" This frequently heard, and factually accurate, reference to Japan reveals two serious misconceptions, that Japan is small and overpopulated. In fact, Japan is larger in area than Great Britain, Italy, or West Germany, and, despite her seventh-ranking position among the nations of the world in population, is facing a labor shortage made more serious by the fact that her birth rate is among the world's lowest.

The four main islands of Japan, together with numberless small islands, form an arc covering roughly the same latitude as the east coast of the United States from Maine to Florida. More than 80 percent of the land area is mountainous, a fact which contributes not only to the highly intensive farming of arable areas, but also to great reliance on the bounty of the sea. The temperate climate is generally congenial to agriculture, permitting winter crops of vegetables except in the snow-covered mountains and the far north. Mineral resources are severely limited, forcing Japan to import essentially all the petroleum, iron ore, and coking coal required by an economy surpassed in size only by the Soviet Union and the United States.

To assert that geographic factors influence the development of a nation is to state the obvious. Yet the measure of this influence is difficult and conducive to controversy. Observers may agree that such dominant factors as the mountainous character of the Japanese islands or the frequency of natural disasters are important; but they differ widely in interpreting the impact of these phenomena.

The relative isolation of the Japanese islands prior to the advent of the steamship and airplane may have had a major impact on the evolution of Japanese culture, as we see in the following selection.

EDWIN O. REISCHAUER,
The United States and Japan,
pp. 101–108 (excerpts)

It is never safe to state unequivocally that certain geographic influences have produced certain specific cultural characteristics. One can so easily find other places in the world where similar geographic conditions had no such result. . . . One geographic factor, however, stands out as a dominant one in Japan's cultural heritage and an element which distinguished Japan from all the other older civilized lands of the world. This factor is isolation. In pre-modern times, no other important group of people consciously participating in the rich culture of the Eurasiatic land mass lived so far removed from all the other civilized peoples. The straits between Japan and Korea are five times as wide as the Straits of Dover, which have had a significant influence in shaping England's history and the character of her people. The distance between Japan and China, the homeland of her civilization, is even greater. Only in recent centuries have peoples of the civilized world come to live at greater distances from the Eurasiatic land mass, and by that time vastly improved techniques of navigation and, now, instantaneous communications have wiped out the factor of isolation.

One obvious influence of isolation on Japan has been the creation of a highly homogeneous race of people there and, what is more important, a very homogeneous culture. The Japanese as a race are primarily a Mongoloid people, as are all the major groups of that part of the world. They differ no more from Koreans and Chinese than Englishmen differ from Frenchmen or Germans. . . .

The Japanese, like all other peoples, are a blend of many diverse elements, but their exact racial composition is, in fact, little known and makes less difference. What is important is that there have been no significant additions of blood to the Japanese race for well over a thousand years. They have had plenty of time to become thoroughly mixed together to form as unified a people as exist anywhere in the world.

Their culture, though repeatedly enriched by foreign borrowings, has also had time to become extremely homogeneous, particularly during the two centuries of Tokugawa isolation [1600–1868]. The Japanese culture of the mid-nineteenth century was perhaps more uniform than the culture of any European country of comparable size. Some observers feel that the Japanese have achieved greater cultural uniformity throughout the length and breadth of the land and throughout the vertical stratifications of their society than has ever been achieved in a country of Japan's size, and they compare Japanese cultural homogeneity to that of a primitive tribe. . . .

Another clear influence of geographic isolation on Japan has been the infrequency of close contacts with foreign lands throughout Japanese history and, conversely, the heavy waves of influence from abroad whenever close contacts did exist. Most other parts of the civilized world have been subject throughout history to a continuous stream of foreign influences, so steady and uniform as to have gone virtually unnoticed most of the time. In Japan, however, the very paucity of such influences at most times meant that, whenever close contacts were feasible, there was likely to be heavy, almost frantic borrowing from abroad. . . .

. . . The alternation of periods of rapid borrowing and comparative isolation has resulted in a clear awareness on the part of the Japanese of the whole process of borrowing. They have been so acutely conscious of this wholesale learning from abroad during certain periods in the past and have so emphasized this aspect of their history that they have helped create the myth that they are nothing but a race of copiers. . . .

While forced by geographic isolation to develop alone more of their own civilization than have most other peoples, they have been overwhelmed with the concept of borrowing from abroad and have, in compensation, emphasized supposed "native" elements more than other nations have. . . . It is as if the French were obsessed with the idea that only that part of their culture which was derived from pre-Roman Gaul was native and labeled all else as foreign borrowings. Such an attempt would send the British back to the druids for their native culture. Naturally, in Japan, it has resulted in a ridiculous emphasis on the primitive and an impossible search in the only hazily known early years of Japanese history for some mysterious source for Japan's later greatness. It has also been the background for a great deal of mystical nonsense about Japan and the Japanese, which has been used to justify a host of absurd political and social doctrines and a particular virulent brand of nationalistic dogma.

There has been, however, one very good result of Japan's consciousness of foreign borrowing. The Japanese take the process of acculturation for granted and are not afraid or ashamed, when circumstances dictate, to borrow whatever they need from abroad. Without the historical example of Japan's heavy borrowing from China a thousand years earlier, it might have been more difficult than it was for the Meiji leaders to conceive the idea of repatterning Japan on Western models and to justify this course of action both to themselves and to their people. Certainly that concept came much more slowly and far more painfully to most of the other peoples of Asia. The Chinese, with their age-old belief that China was the unique civilized land of the world, surrounded by barbarians of varying degrees of inferiority and loyalty to China, found it particularly difficult to accept the idea that anything important could be learned from the West, much less that the Chinese economic and political structure would have to be remade on Western lines. But in Japan it seemed evident that, if the land had been converted into a miniature China in the seventh and eighth centuries, it could be made into an Asiatic England or Germany in the nineteenth. Even today, the concept of another great transformation, dictated this time from abroad, seems less strange and less repugnant to the Japanese than it would to most peoples.

By and large, isolation may have had the curious effect of making the Japanese more ready to accept new things from abroad than were most other peoples—and they certainly have always demonstrated a great enthusiasm for the new—but at the same time isolation has also permitted them to cling more persistently than other nations to the old. The result is Japan's particular form of conservatism, which is the cherishing of the old and outmoded while enthusiastically embracing the new. Perhaps because international friction was less intense in this isolated corner of the globe and the struggle for cultural survival, therefore, less acute, many of the outmoded aspects of Japanese civilization could continue to exist side by side with the new. The Imperial institution itself is a case in point. The Emperors of Japan by the twelfth century had become incongruous survivals of an earlier age. Almost anywhere else in the world, the struggle for national survival would have forced the abandonment of such outgrown forms, but Japanese isolation permitted the coexistence of the old political institutions in theory and the new feudal institutions in practice. . . . The Japanese are like us in that they are always ready and even eager to adopt the new, but at the same time they are very unlike us in their strong tendency to preserve the old and outmoded.

The Prehistoric Period

Despite geographic isolation, the Japanese people are the product of numerous migrations from the mainland of Asia taking place over thousands of years. The exact nature of this process is still a subject of debate and continued research.

Within the past twenty years numerous archaeological finds have testified to the presence of a paleolithic or "prepottery" culture as early as 20,000 B.C. A few fossil bones raise the possibility that an Asian type of Neanderthal man inhabited what is now Japan (prior to its separation from the mainland) as early as 100,000 B.C.

The first clearly defined culture is that of the Jomon (the term is descriptive of the cord impressions found on much of the pottery) extending roughly from 4500 to 250 B.C. These early neolithic peoples, with their distinctive pottery and reliance on hunting, fishing, and food gathering, apparently lived in scattered sites over the greater part of the Japanese islands.

While there is little to link the Jomon in a cultural sense with later ages, the same cannot be said of the succeeding Yayoi * culture (c. 250 B.C.–200 A.D.). Not only were irrigated rice agriculture and the use of bronze and iron features of this culture, but also various pieces of evidence suggest that the Japanese language, the indigenous Shinto religion, and the emergence of hereditary ruling families (one of them probably the source of the present imperial line) began to crystallize during the Yayoi period. The people of the Yayoi culture may with some justification be described as the originators of Japanese culture.

The tomb culture (c. 300–710 A.D.) bridges the gap from prehistory to history. During this period a warrior aristocracy, possibly derived from migrations to Japan from inner Asia via Korea, ruled over a population whose life had changed little from the Yayoi pattern. The innumerable mounded earth tombs which

---

* Named for a precinct in Tokyo where samples of the distinctive pottery of the culture were first unearthed.

give the culture its name (the largest covers a ground area equal to that of the Great Pyramid) testify to the wealth and power of the ruling class.

A vital characteristic of the era was the division of society into hereditary ruling families and a sub-servient class of workers separated into communities by occupation. The chiefs of the ruling families served simultaneously as priests. The ancestors of the ruling families were accorded a semidivine status and were included in the pantheon of "spirits" of the Shinto religion.

This remarkably simple religion has maintained it-self throughout Japanese history, no doubt in large part because of its ties with nature and, hence, the agricultural cycle. In modern times the religion was used by the government to strengthen patriotism and loyalty to the emperor. Although this "State Shinto" was outlawed following Japan's defeat in 1945, the religion itself quietly sustains its place in Japanese life. Even the smallest village boasts a Shinto shrine, and Shinto festivals represent a high point in the lives of the inhabitants. Not only do most weddings include Shinto rituals; but even work on a skyscraper, supertanker, or world exposition site does not begin without a brief ceremony presided over by a priest whose flowing white garments hark back to ancient times. It may even be that the latent power of Shin-toism will, at some future time, again be harnessed to the force of nationalism, for no foreigner can claim a relationship with it, but every Japanese can.

The following selection describes the origin and basic characteristics of this simple religion.

Shintoism

J. E. KIDDER,
Ancient Japan,
pp. 54–56

Gods are known as *kami* in Japan, meaning superior, upper, or top. They are higher forces, above average, but are not credited with extraordinary, miracle-working powers. They are generally benign, intelligent, and endowed with good taste. These gods—the English term is a little too strong, but gods, spirits, deities, or divinities will have to do—preferred the more beautiful and idyllic spots. They inhabited groves of trees, springs, waterfalls, mountaintops, unusual stones, rocky formations and similar places. They resided both in and around these objects and, indeed, in all the phenomena of nature. Seeing life in all objects and forms is known as animism, a kind of nature worship common to numerous primitive peoples. This is the indigenous religion of Japan. There has arisen some mythology for it, the stories of which will be related later, and there are explanations of how the world began, the Japanese islands were created, and the imperial family came to be descended from the Sun Goddess.

In about the fourth century shrine buildings were actually constructed in the sacred groves to certain gods. The gods came to be separated from each other, some recognized as having special qualities and duties, and the rulers appointed priests to tend to the business of the shrines. This obviously kept the shrines under governmental control. All this came about as a matter of course, but no one had yet thought of giving the religion a name. It was the only religion they knew. When another one was brought over from Korea it became necessary to make some distinction. Buddhism, the creed of the Enlightened One, arrived in the sixth century. The adherents to the old religion immediately feared for its existence, and began to take measures to strengthen it. A name was borrowed from China. *Tao*, The Way, was the native animism of China. Using a Chinese way of pronouncing it, the old religion was called *Shinto*, The Way of the Gods, or in the more purely Japanese language, *Kami no Michi*.

All other religions are foreign to Japan. Buddhism, what there is of Taoism, Confucianism and Christianity are to some extent alien even today. Shinto is the taproot. The other religions have never been able to grow anything more than feeder roots. Shinto is in many ways so broad and all-inclusive, and at the same time so vague and nebulous that it has been adaptable to many purposes. It has been made the religion of the state. It has been used to bolster Buddhist ideas by some philosophers who identified Shinto gods with Buddhist gods. It has been useful to excite national efforts during time of war, and to unify the country through the name of the emperor. It can pick up and shed almost anything. In the eighteenth century a serious effort was made to reduce the power of Buddhism and revive the hand of the emperor. Shinto was rigorously purged of everything that it had accumulated during historical centuries, and restored to its pure form. This pure form is its prehistoric—or pre-Buddhist—character. So many cults and theories are claimed for it today that it still remains difficult to describe its prehistoric form. At any rate, in contrast to religions familiar to Westerners, it does not ask for any faith from its believers except in the innate goodness of man, require any effort, or expect any unusual attention to its gods.

Shinto has little speculation in it. There is no moralizing to speak of and it is unconcerned with ethics. It requires prayers, purifications, and ceremonies. As the national religion, everyone in the country before the last war was listed as a shrine member and taxed for the maintenance of the shrines. This brought Christianity into direct conflict with it, but Buddhism has always been able to compromise since it does not necessarily claim to be the only road to salvation. Shinto ritual today takes care of blessings at birth and marriage observances, but Buddhism, with its higher philosophy concerning the soul, cares for the last rites and funeral ceremonies. Shinto generally avoids any connection with the dead and insists on lustrations, or cleansing, after contact with death and disease and other so-called evils. Cleansing was done for a very real reason in ancient times when plagues were common. Today it is symbolically conducted at a shrine to clear the mind of evils, the accumulation of which causes illness and extinction. The ablutions may be performed by washing, bathing, pouring water over oneself, washing out the mouth, throwing rice, and in other ways.

Shinto remains an important element in modern Japanese culture.

DONALD KEENE,
Living Japan, p. 95

Shinto retains its importance even today, in a time of relative adversity for the faith. The newborn baby is still presented at the local shrine to be accepted as a member of the clan (*ujiko*); a wedding most often takes place before the Shinto gods; prayers are addressed to the gods when fields are planted or crops harvested; and whatever feelings of awe and wonder are evoked by the mountainous beauty of the country are channelled into Shinto worship. Most important, perhaps, Shinto remains the national religion of Japan even when all its official connections with the state have been severed. The gods of Shinto are, after all, uniquely Japanese gods, and the religion itself a bond linking all Japanese. There is no Japanese who cannot claim to be a descendant of the gods, and no foreigner who can. A Japanese may hate Buddhism or Christianity, but it is hard for him to hate anything so intimately connected with his country as Shinto. Even the outspoken atheist delights in the Shinto festivals. However weak Shinto may now appear, it holds this attraction; future national leaders, if they so choose, may put its latent power to their own uses.

Legendary History

By the middle of the fifth century one uji or group of powerful families based in the fertile Nara plain near Kyoto had imposed a loose control over central and western Japan and had established its chief as priest and ruler over the area. Direct descendants of these rulers of the Yamato uji have continued to occupy the throne of Japan to the present day.

The earliest accounts of this era are found in two official histories written in the early eighth century. The histories are thought to be generally reliable for the period after 400 A.D.; but the record for earlier times is a mixture of myths, traditions, and Chinese philosophy designed to legitimize the Yamato claim to rule over all Japan. In the accounts the ancestry of the imperial family is traced back through the first emperor, Jimmu, to the sun goddess and beyond to the creators of the very islands of Japan.

The "consciousness of foreign borrowing" noted in our first selection has accorded these histories a place of special importance as sources of information about "pure Japanese culture" as yet unalloyed with Chinese and other "foreign" elements. During the 1930s and early 1940s, when ultranationalism reached its peak, it was dangerous for a Japanese to question the authenticity of the documents, even to the idea of a ruling line of heavenly descent. Ironically, therefore, these histories had a far greater impact in the twentieth century than at any previous time.

The following selection from the larger of the two histories, the *Nihongi* (or *Nihon Shoki*) of 720 A.D., reveals several characteristic features. The central figures are the sun goddess Amaterasu and her troublesome brother, the wind god Sosa-no-o. Amaterasu is, of course, the progenitor of the imperial line. Her brother may have served the same role for the rulers of an uji which the Yamato uji defeated and drove to a remote section of the country. By this interpretation the myths of a defeated group were integrated with those of the Yamato line in a manner designed to prove the superiority of the Yamato. The evil deeds attributed to the unruly wind god are also of interest. Obviously, destruction of the complex and vital irrigated rice fields constituted a most serious crime. Likewise, the acts of defilement would be reprehensible from the viewpoint of the Shinto emphasis on purity and cleanliness. The withdrawal of the sun goddess to a cave is presumed to be a solar-eclipse myth.

NIHONGI,
pp. 40–45

After this Sosa-no-o's [the wind god's] behavior was exceedingly rude. In what way? Amaterasu [the sun goddess] had made august rice-fields of Heavenly narrow rice-fields and Heavenly long rice-fields. Then Sosa-no-o, when the seed was sown in spring, broke down the divisions between the plots of rice, and in autumn let loose the Heavenly piebald colts, and made them lie down in the midst of the rice-fields. Again, when he saw that Amaterasu was about to celebrate the feast of first-fruits, he secretly voided excrement in the New Palace. Moreover, when he saw that Amaterasu was in her sacred weaving hall, engaged in weaving the garments of the Gods, he flayed a piebald colt of Heaven, and breaking a hole in the roof-tiles of the hall, flung it in. Then Amaterasu started with alarm, and wounded herself with the shuttle. Indignant at this, she straightway entered the Rock-cave of Heaven, and having fastened the Rock-door, dwelt there in seclusion. Therefore constant darkness prevailed on all sides, and the alternation of night and day was unknown.

Then the eighty myriads of Gods met on the bank of the Tranquil River of Heaven, and considered in what manner they should supplicate her. Accordingly Omoi-Kane no Kami, with profound device and far-reaching thought, at length gathered long-singing birds [roosters]of the Eternal Land and made them utter their prolonged cry to one another. Moreover he made Taji-kara-o to stand beside the Rock-door. Then Ame no Koyane no Mikoto, ancestor of the Nakatomi, and Futo-dama no Mikoto, ancestor of the Imibe,* dug up a five-hundred branched true Sakaki tree of the Heavenly

---

* The Nakatomi and Imibe were powerful families in the Yamato uji. Like the Imperial family, they are provided with supernatural ancestors. Many of the other gods mentioned serve the same purpose for other great families. [Ed.]

Mount Kagu. On its upper branches they hung an august five-hundred string of Yasaka jewels. On the middle branches they hung an eight-hand [length] mirror.

On its lower branches they hung blue soft offerings and white soft offerings. Then they recited their liturgy together.

Moreover Ama no Uzume no Mikoto, ancestress of the Sarume, took in her hand a spear wreathed with Eulalia grass, and standing before the door of the Rock-cave of Heaven, skillfully performed a mimic dance. She took, moreover, the true Sakaki tree of the Heavenly Mount Kagu, and made of it a head-dress, she took club-moss and made of it braces, she kindled fires, she placed a tub bottom upwards [to dance on], and gave forth a divinely-inspired utterance.

Now Amaterasu heard this, and said:—"Since I have shut myself up in the Rock-cave, there ought surely to be continual night in the Central Land of fertile reed-plains. How then can Ama no Uzume no Mikoto be so jolly?" So with her august hand, she opened for a narrow space the Rock-door and peeped out. Then Tajikara-o forthwith took Amaterasu by the hand, and led her out. Upon this the Gods Ame no Koyane no Mikoto and Futo-dama no Mikoto at once drew a limit by means of a new straw rope and begged her not to return again (into the cave).

After this all the Gods put the blame on Susa-no-o, and imposed on him a fine of one thousand tables [as an offering], and so at length chastised him. They also had his hair plucked out, and made him therewith expiate his guilt.

PART II. THE IMPORTATION OF CHINESE CULTURE (550–794)

Buddhism

As we have seen, the Japanese people are a product of migrations from the Asian mainland. In the mid-sixth century the Yamato leaders initiated and controlled a vigorous induction of Chinese culture.

The impact of Chinese high culture on Japan was so great that Japan came to be regarded by both Chinese and, later, Westerners as simply a cultural offshoot of China. As will be demonstrated in a later selection (pp. 43–49) this strongly overstates the case. However, there is no doubt that the upper classes in particular were rapidly and deeply affected after the sixth century by Chinese theory and practice in almost every aspect of human activity from governmental organization to a system of writing.

Many factors combined to bring about this crucial development in Japanese history. These included a need on the part of the Yamato leaders for more effective means of government to consolidate and extend their rule, the achievement by this time of a foundation of organizational and technical skills sufficient to sustain the sophisticated cultural patterns of China, and a profound admiration for the religion then in the heyday of its influence in China—Buddhism.

Though Buddhism was not to reach the common people in Japan until the twelfth century, its early impact on the upper classes was deep and broad.

The following selection surveys the development of Buddhism from its introduction to the present and concludes with an assessment of its significance for the Japanese today. Particular note should be taken of the discussion of Zen Buddhism, a sect which has had a profound impact on the arts but neither in the past nor the present has had the tremendous influence claimed for it by some Western enthusiasts.

DONALD KEENE,
Living Japan, pp. 95–108

When Buddhism was introduced to Japan by Korean priests at the end of the sixth century, it was not only a far more complex and satisfying religion than Shinto, but it also was the vehicle which brought the great civilizations of India and China to Japan. As the first world religion it had spread in all directions from its place of origin in northern India, and raised splendid temples and monasteries in great cities and in the desert oases of Central Asia. The most brilliant men of a dozen countries had devoted themselves to compiling volumes of explanations of the sacred texts, and a prodigal outpouring of painting and sculpture filled innumerable halls and grottoes. It is not surprising that the Japanese rulers, accustomed only to the unadorned, rustic shrines of Shinto, a religion which at the time could not boast a single line of scripture, were overawed by Buddhism and eagerly sought to acquire a grasp of its principles.

Buddhist texts were a medium of instruction in the Chinese language, a knowledge of which unlocked for the Japanese, still living under primitive conditions, the treasury of learning of the world's most highly civilized people. Just as many centuries later Japanese were to attend Christian churches and listen to sermons in English as a means of improving their linguistic abilities, so their ancestors in the seventh century eagerly conned Buddhist writings for help with their Chinese. Shinto, the old religion, was cast into the shade, and by the middle of the seventh century there was an emperor who "honored the religion of Buddha and despised the Way of the Gods."

The Buddhism originally introduced to Japan was a religion of monks who devoted themselves to an intensive study of extremely difficult texts. Such philosophical and theological studies had a long history in India and China, but in Japan, where the ability to read was itself a recent acquisition, it was still much too early to hope for real understanding of the sacred books. A handful of learned men in the monasteries pondered such doctrines as the dialectics of negation or the metaphysics of the harmonious whole, but only a few relatively simple ideas reached the lay Buddhists of the seventh and eighth centuries. Chief of these was the obligation of the ruler to honor and practice the Buddhist law. The piety of the court was most often expressed in the erection of temples honoring the Buddha. The city of Nara, the capital of Japan in the eighth century, is still dominated by the hails of worship and pagodas first raised at that time. The most famous single monument of Nara Buddhism was the Great Image of Buddha, completed in 749 A.D. This bronze statue, over fifty feet in height, is still impressive, though hopelessly disfigured by earthquakes and other disasters.

Many varieties of Buddhism were introduced during the following centuries. From the ninth to the twelfth centuries esoteric teachings predominated. These purported to be doctrines of so lofty a nature that they could only be transmitted by a teacher directly to his chosen pupils. The words, bodily attitude and mind of the worshipper, all had to be attuned to this demanding religion by the recitation of sacred spells, the performance of ritual gestures, and a concentration on the mysteries of the faith. Only initiates could hope to comprehend the full glories of esoteric Buddhism, though works of art could suggest the meaning of the faith to larger numbers of believers. Court ladies used fans painted with scenes from the sacred books in order to cool themselves and derive spiritual benefit at the same time. It became fashionable for members of the aristocracy to "leave the world" as priests and nuns; however, in the interests of beauty—the passionate concern of the age—only the tips of a nun's locks were trimmed instead of her head being shaved in the required way. The Buddhism of the time was suitable to a society in which aesthetic considerations were paramount, and bad taste the most unforgivable sin.

As yet Buddhism held no appeal for the common people. From time to time the court encouraged Buddhism worship in the homes or ordered the erection of temples in the distant countryside, but the Shinto gods were much closer to the people than Buddha and his bodhisattvas living in their foreign-looking temples. Even had the ordinary folk wished to gain enlightenment, they could not have easily gone along with the Nara monks in believing that the outer world was a mere creation of the mind, nor could they have hoped to be accepted as chosen disciples of the esoteric faith.

During the twelfth century almost incessant warfare, earthquakes, and other natural disasters led to the appearance of a new type of Buddhism, one destined to win the allegiance of the vast majority of Japanese. This was the Pure Land Buddhism. It taught that the world had entered its last degenerate days and that men could no longer achieve salvation by their own efforts. Only by imploring the help of Amida, an incarnation of Buddha who had once vowed to save all men, was it possible to be reborn in paradise after death. All that was necessary was to call on Amida with the single phrase *Namu Amida Butsu*. Early missionaries spread this teaching to remote villages by dancing through the streets singing the saving invocation. Anyone could understand and practice this kind of Buddhism. It gave the ordinary farmer as great a chance of salvation as the most learned monk, or perhaps an even greater one:

some adherents of Pure Land Buddhism went so far as to claim that a wicked man would be saved sooner than a priest, because a priest was likely to take a false pride in the importance of his own merits, whilst the wicked (or ignorant) man had no choice but to trust in Amida. No longer was it necessary to study the sacred texts of Buddhism; a single invocation of *Namu Amida Butsu* was enough. This sounds very simple, but it meant that a man had to humble himself to the extent of admitting that he was a nonentity incapable of saving himself. Moreover, in return for Amida's grace in admitting him to the Pure Land, a man was expected to give up everything, even his life.

It made sense to people living in a world torn by disorders when a religion taught them that this world was an evil place and the only existence which counted was the one in Amida's paradise. They eagerly accepted the new religion without, however, forsaking the Shinto gods whose help they still needed. No matter how confident a farmer might be of rebirth in the Pure Land, he had to worry about his crops while on earth, and Amida promised nothing for this life. It thus came about quite naturally that the two religions, so contradictory in their tenets, were simultaneously believed in by the mass of Japanese, who found divine help in both.

The widespread adoption of Pure Land Buddhism meant that Buddhism had at last become thoroughly Japanese. No longer was it necessary to study Sanskrit or Chinese in order to read the sacred books. The ignorant farmer could call Amida's name or sing hymns of praise written in simple Japanese. An even more pronouncedly Japanese character was lent to Buddhism by the priest Nichiren (1222–1292), who preached that Japan was the land where the true teachings of the Buddha were to be revived. His followers later claimed that Japan better deserved the name of Buddha's land than either India or China, simply because Nichiren was a Japanese. Nichiren himself rose to prominence by his repeated prophecies of disaster, which seemed confirmed in the worst way when the Mongol invasions menaced Japan at the end of the thirteenth century. He taught the importance of enduring suffering, a doctrine which his followers have put into practice by braving all opposition in order to propagandize their beliefs. Unlike some Buddhists who calmly endure suffering, Nichiren Buddhists actively court it. In their determination that their faith shall prevail, they constantly try to "break and subdue" members of other sects. Even today one may often hear late at night the beat of a drum and voices crying *Namu Myoho Renge-kyo* (Hail to the Lotus Sutra), the invocation preferred by Nichiren's followers. In the 1930's Nichiren priests frequently associated themselves with ultranationalistic movements, thus carrying their righteous determination to the field of political action. Their names still figure prominently in committees organized to "restore" Japan by re-establishing the old virtues. The martial character of Nichiren Buddhism has made it congenial to Japanese men of action.

Another type of Buddhism which originally drew its strength from the samurai class was Zen, a sect destined to exert a much wider influence than Nichiren Buddhism. Zen placed emphasis on discipline and meditation at every moment in the believer's life. The Zen masters did not abandon the sacred texts of Buddhism, as is sometimes stated, but insisted instead that they were there to be used. The believer had to lead the life of the Buddha, and the texts could help him in this. One sect of Zen developed a technique of presenting students with problems which could not be solved by ordinary logical processes, but required a flash of insight which might lead to enlightenment. The priest sitting for hours in meditation might also be startled into such an awakening by a sudden blow. But Dôgen (1200–1253), the greatest of the Zen masters, taught that obtaining sudden enlightenment was not the important thing; sitting in meditation itself could lead to a gradual and complete realization of the Buddha-nature within each man.

The insistence of Zen doctrine on self-reliance put it at opposite poles from the Pure Land sects. The place of honor in Zen temples was shared by the Buddha with images of the Zen masters of the past, ordinary men who by their own powers had realized their Buddha-nature. Zen's appeal for the military dictators of Japan in the thirteenth and fourteenth centuries was such that it developed from a discipline to a major religion with huge monasteries and properties. Many of them survive today, splendid clusters of temple buildings and gardens which are marked by a bare simplicity and cleanliness natural in those who must lead the lives of the Buddha at every moment. The severity of the Zen monastery had its equivalent in many arts: in landscape gardening, where some famous gardens (notably those of the Ryoanji and Daitokuji temples in Kyoto) consist entirely of stones and sand, as if growing plants would be an unneccessary and untidy embellishment; in the Nô theater, where all plays take place against the same backdrop of a single painted pine, and the props are no more than stylized renderings of the objects portrayed; in landscape painting, where monochromes took the place of the brilliantly colored images favored by artists of earlier schools of Buddhism; and in the tea ceremony, an art which was almost entirely developed by Zen monks. In each of these arts the essentials, the bare bones, are what matter, just as in Zen doctrine realization of the Buddha-nature rather than the quiddities of theology was emphasized. There is deliberate understatement, reflecting not the poverty of minds which lack the imagination to handle a variety of rich effects but the discipline of those which reject a profusion of ornamentation in favor of a few significant lines. . . .

The Japanese Buddhist sects, despite their wide differences in doctrine, have generally—with the notable exception of Nichiren's sect—managed to get along amicably. Most Japanese, in any case, have only a rudimentary grasp of the complexities of their particular sect of Buddhism. In some parts of the country, for example, the rural population is registered mainly with Zen temples as the result of the command issued by some local potentate centuries ago. For most of these Zen believers, however, sitting in meditation would be as unthinkable as performing a mass would be for the lay Catholic. Their only connection with the temple to which they belong comes from the necessity of holding memorial services for the dead. The priest of the temple himself, though he undoubtedly once concerned himself with Zen doctrines, is more likely now to be preoccupied by parish activities or by the affairs of his own household. This does not mean that he is a bad priest, but that the discipline expected of a true Zen monk cannot be observed by a parish priest.

Virtually all Japanese are Buddhists, at least in name, but few young people possess any knowledge of their religion. The devotion seems to have petered out which as late as the 1890's impelled thousands of women to offer their hair to make a cable 360 feet long and strong enough to lift the timbers of the new Eastern Honganji Temple in Kyoto. Children today are barely taught to distinguish between Shinto shrines (where they must clap their hands at the altar) and Buddhist temples (where they bow in silence). With a handful of exceptions, the young men who today elect to become Buddhist priests are the sons of other priests and have decided that the priesthood offers them the best chance of making a living. There are universities in Tokyo and Kyoto established by the various Buddhist sects to train men for the priesthood, but the students tend to be resigned to their careers rather than eager.

A few young men, however, are genuinely desirous

of becoming priests, and this is a hopeful sign for Buddhism. Little in Japanese life encourages them if they have a religious bent. For hundreds of years Japanese intellectuals have been attacking the Buddhist priesthood as lazy and incompetent, often with considerable justice. The popular writers of today are apt to decry religion as an "opiate of the masses," and an identification is invariably made between Buddhism and superstition. Many young priests are ashamed of their calling and wear Western clothes whenever possible, clamping felt hats on their shaven heads to conceal their identity.

A traveler arriving in Japan today from other Buddhist nations—Ceylon, Thailand or Burma—cannot but be struck by the religious apathy. Unlike the prime ministers of those countries, Japanese statesmen do not proclaim their Buddhist piety, nor do they refer to the teachings of Buddha in their public addresses. The achievements of the great Japanese Buddhist teachers have been deleted from textbooks, and the secular nature of Japanese education is stressed. Even the names of the principal sects are unknown to many university students. Nor does Buddhism retain its former hold on farmers. In Southeast Asia enormous crowds of devout believers will eagerly press forward for a glimpse of any holy relics displayed; in Japan farmer-pilgrims are likely to be sightseers in the temples, shepherded from one "national treasure" to the next. Some writers and artists still treat Buddhist themes in their works, but usually as outsiders looking on with friendly curiosity rather than with the conviction of believers. The apathy extends to the monasteries, originally built to hold a hundred or more priests but now housing a mere five or six; in the evening the monks are more likely to gather around a television set than to read the holy books. Thanks to various dispensations of the 1870's the visitor arriving at some great temple in Kyoto may be just in time to see the butcher present his weekly bill, or he may interrupt a priest playing with his children. It is small wonder that travelers from Southeast Asia, where meat-eating, married priests are inconceivable, refuse to believe that the Japanese are really Buddhists.

Most Buddhist temples in Japan are today in poor economic shape. The land reforms after 1945 deprived them of the chief source of their income. Today the larger temples depend in part on the admission fees charged for the privilege of examining their treasures. The central temples of a sect also receive contributions from each of the affiliated temples throughout the country. Rich men are sometimes persuaded to contribute to fund-raising drives; one sees their names and the amount they have given written on signs outside the temples. The situation is much worse in remote temples, where sometimes it is impossible to find a successor when the old priest dies. Temples in scenic spots have taken to renting their premises for meetings and picnics or even serve as hotels. Other temples, less likely to attract tourists, have become lodgings for poor students, or hang signs at their gates announcing that lessons in calligraphy or flower arrangement can be arranged. The gardens of such temples are likely to be overgrown, the paintings on the paper screens peeling and discolored, and weeds three feet high grow from the tops of the gates. The casual visitor is stared at by small children in the courtyard, and when the priest's wife appears from the kitchen in an apron she timidly asks for the entrance fee. If anything commends the temple, she will have memorized the description from some old guide-book, and as she leads the visitor through the dilapidated rooms to reach some statue or painting, she hastily shuts doors on rooms where clothes are being mended or bedding still lies on the floor.

Temples are generally deserted except during the Bon festival in August and while funeral services are actually in progress. Some temples have annual festivals, but they differ from Shinto festivals in that they are spectacles, and not celebrations in which the crowd may join. The Nigatsu-do (Hall of the Second Moon), a temple in Nara, actually has a stage where the priests perform at *Mizutori*, "the water-dipping." This ancient ceremony was originally a mass confessional of the priests, but today it features weird "Tartar" dances and ritual. A crowd of spectators surrounds the hall, peering through lattice-work windows at the priests who pass by circling the main altar in the semi-darkness, chanting spells in a mysterious language, and pounding with their wooden shoes on the floor boards. Bashô described it:

Mizutori ya	Water-dipping rite—
Kôri no sô no	The clatter of the pattens
Kutsu no oto	Of the cloistered priests.

It is a haunting sight to see the priests, clad in Central-Asian robes, performing their incantations in the flickering torchlight. At the conclusion they rush forward onto the temple stage and dance to wild rhythms swinging great brands and showering cascades of sparks on the spectators below. The water-dipping is now a relatively minor part of the ceremony, though once the sacred water was believed to be a magical elixir.

The Buddhist ceremonial in which the public takes the greatest part is the Bon festival, a kind of Feast of the Dead held in August. Most Japanese, wherever they may reside, go back to their ancestral home at least for this one occasion to decorate the family graves with flowers. The dead are said to return at this season, and a visit to the graves is therefore especially important. In some villages along the coast the souls of the dead are sent away after the festival in tiny boats bearing lights that disappear at sea.

Everywhere in Japan there are Bon dances. One may see them in empty lots in the cities, where a scratchy phonograph record blasts out the musical accompaniment over loudspeakers, and the dancers wear sport shirts and printed summer frocks. In the country, especially in a remote region like the Valley of Kiso, the dances preserve something of the traditions of the past. At dusk the people begin to gather in the main street of the town, forming a circle. All wear Japanese dress, or at least elements of it, and tie a towel around their head. One person takes up the refrain, a somewhat bawdy ballad, and the dancers perform to it the four or five simple movements of the dance. The burden of the song passes from one man or woman to another, and gradually the circle of dancers grows larger, until the whole town seems to be dancing under the bright August moon.

Little in the Bon festival dances suggests their Buddhist origins, and some scholars even assert that they are completely secular. Japanese tend to think of Buddhism as a gloomy religion of the dead, but the liveliness of these dances accords poorly with this belief.

Buddhism, for all its present decline, has indelibly colored the Japanese way of thinking. For example, the impermanence of this world, perhaps the most frequently reiterated theme in Buddhist writings, gave rise to the peculiarly Japanese concept of beauty. The priest Kenkô wrote in the fourteenth century, "Were we to live on forever, then indeed would men not feel the pity of things. Truly the beauty of life is its uncertainty." The Japanese came to prize perishability, a trait which Lafcadio Hearn once termed "the genius of Japanese civilization." He wrote, in *Kokoro*, "Generally speaking, we construct for endurance, the Japanese for impermanency. Few things for common use are made in Japan with a view to durability. The straw sandals worn out and replaced at each stage of a journey; the robe consisting of a few simple widths loosely stitched together for wearing, and unstitched again for washing; the fresh chopsticks served to each new guest at a hotel; the light *shoji* frames serving at once for windows and walls, and repapered twice a year; the matting renewed every autumn—all these are but random examples of countless small things in daily life that illustrate the national contentment with impermanency."

To bewail the passing of things or the changes that time brings is common to many peoples and literatures (and may be found in Japan too), but to discover in impermanence the essence of beauty is characteristic of Japan. The fact that the cherry blossom is considered the Japanese national flower underlines this point. The cherry blossoms are in their glory for at most three or four days, and during the rest of the year the tree is an utter nuisance. It produces thousands of minuscule inedible cherries which must be swept away; it is such a great favorite with insects, particularly caterpillars, that by the end of summer one is well advised to carry an umbrella under its boughs; and it loses its leaves long before the other trees. Yet for a few days of enjoyment the Japanese not only tolerate the cherry tree, but plant it everywhere and genuinely love it. Indeed, if the blossoms stayed longer on the boughs (like plum blossoms, for example,), the tree would undoubtedly be less highly prized because less impermanent. The Japanese soldier during the war liked to compare himself to the cherry blossoms falling after a brief moment of glory, rather than to the chrysanthemums blooming steadfastly.

Small children are taught the Buddhist lesson of impermanence. The poem from which the Japanese have traditionally learned their syllabary (it contains each of the forty-seven syllables) begins

Iro ha nihohedo	Though the color be fragrant
Chirinuru wo	The flower will fall:
Waga yo tarezo	Who in this world of ours
Tsune naramu...	Will last forever?

The child at first unthinkingly parrots the syllables, but something of the poem's content will sooner or later affect him. Not only the poem, of course, but innumerable other works of Japanese literature confirm this view of life. No matter how violently a Japanese may oppose Buddhism, he has been unalterably tinged by its philosophy, much in the way that an Italian, even an atheist, will have been by Catholicism. Because most children receive no religious instruction today, they are likely to be ignorant of everything they see in a temple. Yet they will almost instinctively appreciate the beauty of works of art which may baffle foreigners, and in their speech they inevitably have recourse to the many words which Buddhism has given the Japanese language. Tough young men today do not, it is true, blame their misfortunes on the sins of a previous existence, but they seem to share in the fatalism which is said to come from the Buddhist doctrine of *karma*.

Today the Buddhist altar is empty in some Japanese houses. In others the daily offering of cooked rice and water is neglected. But in millions of houses the prescribed observances are faithfully continued, and every present received by the family is first placed before the Buddha. Carpenters have had to find ways of fitting a Buddhist altar into some of the newly built Tokyo houses, though no need for one had been anticipated by the young and up-to-date owners. Indeed, one of the most striking features of Buddhism in Japan during the past few centuries has been how close it has frequently seemed to destruction, and how each time— often for no apparent reason—it has managed to survive. When one visits some old deserted temple, where there is not even a resident priest, it is easy to visualize it crumbling into mouldering timbers as the hands of its statues drop off, and the gold leaf flakes from the altar. Yet the traveler who returns years later, expecting to find a desolate wilderness, may equally well see new tiles on the roof and fresh gilding on the images. The Buddhist cycle, after all, insists not only on decay but regeneration.

Religion Adapts to the Modern Scene

The following passages taken from an article in a recent issue of a popular Japanese magazine illustrate both the continuing life of religion and its adjustment to the concerns of an affluent industrialized society. Traffic safety and college-entrance examinations loom much larger in the lives of today's Japanese than the hope for good harvests.

SHUKAN BUNSHUN

Although Japan is still crowded with [Buddhist] temples and [Shinto] shrines all over the country, gods and Buddha have long been dead in the minds of most Japanese.

The first few days every January is an exceptional period, however. During the period, millions of Japanese, men and women, young and old, troop to temples and shrines.

But the sudden and momentary pilgrimages are hardly an expression of a religious spirit. They simply want their gods to do something good for them in the new year.

Temples and shrines have been flexible enough to cater to the wishes of these January worshipers. There are all kinds of religious institutions that suit your wishes.

In the old days when the ox-cart was the fastest means of transportation, no temples promised traffic safety as a reward for worshiping.

But today when dozens of persons get killed in traffic accidents, across the country it's natural for considerate temples and shrines to serve drivers. . . .

Blessings for traffic safety have become so popular that even the 12-century-old Kasuga Shrine in Nara takes good care of drivers.

Among the 1,500,000 worshipers visiting the shrine in January are several thousand drivers who want their cars blessed for traffic safety.

For most Japanese youths, studying at one of the better universities is an important and almost indispensable stepping stone to rising higher in society.

So youths favor the Kameido Tenjin Shrine, dedicated to Sugawara Michizane, one of the greatest scholars in the 9th century. Over 150,000 youths throng the shrine in January alone to pray for success in entrance examinations to universities they want to enter.

Anxious parents are also earnest worshipers there. . . .

Prince Shotoku—the Sinophile

The desire to consolidate and extend the power of the Yamato state was a major reason for the importation of Chinese civilization and, to this end, strenuous efforts were made during the seventh and eighth centuries to duplicate most elements of the elaborate governmental system of China. This was no simple task, since China at that time was by far the most powerful and sophisticated civilization in the world.

A central role in the early stages of this development was played by Prince Shotoku, who served as regent from 592 until his death in 622. Prince Shotoku is one of the relatively few figures from Japanese history who is known to all Japanese today; his face appears on much of the paper currency now in circulation.

The selection below is taken from a document which was assumed until very recently to have been written by Shotoku as a sort of constitution to guide the establishment of a Chinese-style central government, though it may, in fact, have been written some years after his death as a tribute to his memory.

Despite the reference to Buddhism in Article II the content of the "Constitution" is drawn almost entirely from Confucian philosophy. This simply reflects the role of Confucianism in China where it had provided the basic philosophy of government and ethics since 200 B.C. The references to "harmony," "decorous behaviour," and "distinctions of rank" represent key features of the Confucian ethic. The assertion that obedience to the emperor is as natural and vital as "Earth's" submission to "Heaven" not only states a fundamental premise of Confucianism but also demonstrates the practical value of the philosophy to an as yet disunited society.

NIHONGI,
pp. 129–133

I. Harmony is to be valued, and an avoidance of wanton opposition to be honoured. All men are influenced by class-feelings, and there are few who are intelligent. Hence there are some who disobey their lords and fathers, or who maintain feuds with the neighbouring villages. But when those above are harmonious and those below are friendly, and there is concord in the discussion of business, right views of things spontaneously gain acceptance. Then what is there which cannot be accomplished! . . .

II. Sincerely reverence the three treasures. The three treasures, viz. Buddha, the Law and the Priesthood, are the final refuge of the four generated beings, and are the supreme objects of faith in all countries. What man in what age can fail to reverence this law? Few men are utterly bad. They may be taught to follow it. But if they do not betake them to the three treasures, wherewithal shall their crookedness be made straight?

III. When you receive the Imperial commands, fail not scrupulously to obey them. The lord is Heaven, the vassal is Earth. Heaven overspreads, and Earth upbears. When this is so, the four seasons follow their due course, and the powers of Nature obtain their efficacy. If the Earth attempted to overspread, Heaven would simply fall in ruin. Therefore is it that when the lord speaks, the vassal listens; when the superior acts, the inferior yields compliance. Consequently when you receive the Imperial commands, fail not to carry them out scrupulously. Let there be a want of care in this matter, and ruin is the natural consequence.

IV. The Ministers and functionaries should make decorous behaviour their leading principle, for the leading principle of the government of the people consists in decorous behaviour. If the superiors do not behave with decorum, the inferiors are disorderly: if inferiors are wanting in proper behaviour, there must necessarily be offences. Therefore it is that when lord and vassal behave with propriety, the distinctions of rank are not confused: when the people behave with propriety, the Government of the Commonwealth proceeds of itself.

V. Ceasing from gluttony and abandoning covetous desires, deal impartially with the suits which are submitted to you. Of complaints brought by the people there are a thousand in one day. If in one day there are so many, how many will there be in a series of years? If the man who is to decide suits at law makes gain his ordinary motive, and hears causes with a view to receiving bribes, then will the suits of the rich man be like a stone flung into water, while the plaints of the poor will resemble water cast upon a stone. Under these circumstances the poor man will not know whither to betake himself. Here too there is a deficiency in the duty of the Minister.

VI. Chastise that which is evil and encourage that which is good. This was the excellent rule of antiquity. Conceal not, therefore, the good qualities of others, and fail not to correct that which is wrong when you see it. Flatterers and deceivers are a sharp weapon for the overthrow of the State, and a pointed sword for the destruction of the people. Sycophants are also fond, when they meet, of dilating to their superiors on the errors of their inferiors; to their inferiors, they censure the faults of their superiors. Men of this kind are all wanting in fidelity to their lord, and in benevolence towards the people. From such an origin great civil disturbances arise. . . .

IX. Good faith is the foundation of right. In everything let there be good faith, for in it there surely consists the good and the bad, success and failure. If the lord and the vassal observe good faith one with another, what is there which cannot be accomplished? If the lord and the vassal do not observe good faith towards one another, everything without exception ends in failure.

X. Let us cease from wrath, and refrain from angry looks. Nor let us be resentful when others differ from us. For all men have hearts, and each heart has its own leanings. Their right is our wrong, and our right is their wrong. We are not unquestionably sages, nor are they unquestionably fools. Both of us are simply ordinary men. How can any one lay down a rule by which to distinguish right from wrong? For we are all, one with another, wise and foolish, like a ring which has no end. Therefore, although others give way to anger, let us on the contrary dread our own faults, and though we alone may be in the right, let us follow the multitude and act like them.

XI. Give clear appreciation to merit and demerit, and deal out to each its sure reward or punishment. In these days, reward does not attend upon merit, nor punishment upon crime. Ye high functionaries who have charge of public affairs, let it be your task to make clear rewards and punishments. . . .

XVI. Let the people be employed (in forced labour) at seasonable times. This is an ancient and excellent rule. Let them be employed, therefore, in the winter months, when they are at leisure. But from Spring to Autumn, when they are engaged in agriculture or with the mulberry trees, the people should not be so employed. For if they do not attend to agriculture, what will they have to eat? if they do not attend to the mulberry trees, what will they do for clothing? . . .

Life During the Nara Period

By the beginning of the eighth century the process of Sinicization had brought great changes to the Nara Plain. Imposing monasteries and temples dotted the plain and surrounding hills. Many of these buildings still stand today. The hordes of tourists who visit them are reminded not only of their significance to the history of Japan but also of their status as the finest surviving examples of architecture from the brilliant T'ang Dynasty of China, for, ironically, the Chinese originals after which these buildings were patterned have long since been destroyed.

Another visible evidence of Chinese influence could be clearly seen in the appearance of the rice paddies. What had once been a formless jumble of paddies of all sizes and shapes now became a gridiron of identical rectangles. The Chinese had devised this system to ease the process of assessing and collecting the grain tax for the central government. Even today it is possible to estimate the reach of government power in the eighth century by noting the points at which this rectilinear pattern gives way to forms dictated more by nature than political theory.

No doubt these achievements seemed minor when compared to the magnificence of Nara, Japan's first capital city. Completed in 712, this city duplicated on a reduced scale the wonders of Changan, the capital of T'ang China. Among the numerous temples one, the Great Buddha Hall, was so massive that today, in a version one-third smaller than the original, it is claimed to be the largest wooden structure in the world.

To anyone seeing only the capital, it might have seemed that the Japanese had all but duplicated the brilliance of Chinese civilization within little more than a century of effort. However, as we see in the following selection, even a short journey would have revealed how little the changes had affected the lives of the common people.

LANGDON WARNER,
The Enduring Art of Japan,
pp. 7–16

What, then, was the outward look of the capital city of Nara, and what were the craftman's surroundings in that short eighth century that bulks so big in Japanese history? The town of Nara was laid out like a grid as was Ch'ang-an, the contemporary capital of the T'ang dynasty in China. In Nara streets were broader than they are today, for on one or two of the main avenues three bullcarts could go abreast. But they were often sloughs, and the man afoot chose to walk under dripping eaves or to scrape against a mud wall or a quick-set hedge rather than plow down the middle.

For lack of draft animals, workers bore their own burdens on carrying poles on their shoulders. No wheeled vehicles were seen, except when the aristocracy passed on two-wheeled bullcarts, hooded and curtained like prairie schooners. These whined and groaned on wooden axles, a sound that has become part of the trite furniture of the classical poet and is reproduced with archaeological accuracy, even today, when an Emperor is borne with antique ceremony to his tomb. But the huge bulks of building timber, on their way to the temples and palaces under construction, were pulled on log rollers by bulls or by long lines of men on the ropes.

On the slopes of the hills, four miles apart to east and west in Nara city, were great monasteries set in their parks, and one could see their pagodas and groves from the rice fields and from the city streets. Midway between these temples lay the palace buildings, recently tiled in place of the old thatch, and with corner posts painted red. They were walled about, however, with rammed clay walls topped by tiles, so that the humble never saw the courtyards or the gardens.

Except in winter, the city stank with sewage, for Nara plain is hot and flat, but the odor of it could probably not be compared with the stench of the close European town of that day. The Japanese were, even then, ceremonially clean in their persons, which was emphatically not true of Europeans.

Once clear of Nara, the tracks narrowed to footpaths, unless one chose a road recently widened and mended for the passage of nobility in bullcarts. On it were unending streams of burden carriers fetching produce to town. But the line must scatter when a cavalier came by with his mounted men and his men afoot. He took for himself the beaten track, and other wayfarers must plunge into the mud of the bordering paddy fields or take a beating.

The messenger from the court to the provinces, carrying letters to some distant government, was a knight riding a high wooden saddle with immense scoops for stirrups. He went in silk and fine hemp cloth, tan colored in summer, for the road, but in his painted boxes, carried on shoulder poles by the escort, was plate armor of lacquered leather with iron fitments and a store of food for the journey and lacquered trays and bowls to serve it. He would find no inns and must put up at the houses of such rural nobles as lived along his route and, best of all, at temples when he found them. Failing either of these, the headman of a village was warned in advance by runner, and, when the knight reached the end of his day's stage, the farmhouse would be garnished and the peasant host and family moved out to sleep with the neighbors.

No fine foods or luxuries could be got at such places but there was hot water, and fodder could be requisitioned for the beasts. Tea was a rarity occasionally imported and not yet grown in Japan. Rice and barley or millet could usually be supplied, but the knight brought his own wine and flat dumpling cakes or salt bean paste. He and his followers often had fresh fish, but could be sure of nothing more than bowls of steamed millet, flavored perhaps with morsels of salt fish.

At this time, when Buddhism was spreading among the upper classes with increasing speed, meat eating was frowned upon and hunting a sin. However, on the road, necessity knows no law. The fare was often varied by venison, wild pig, a pheasant from the villagers' snares, or an occasional duck. The further one left behind the dominant great temples of Nara and their ever-present clergy the more generally one saw meat being eaten when it could be got. The well-found traveler took with him a leash of hunting dogs and a perch of falcons, to beguile the journey and fill the pot.

Except for hilltops, shrine precincts, and the boundaries between fields, the countryside for some two or three days out of Nara was, before the middle of the eighth century, already stripped of the best timber. But if the traveler headed north, he came on the third day to forests where he had dread of wild beasts and evil spirits of the woods. As a matter of fact, there was little to harm, though wolves did come down so far when snow was deep in the north. Monkeys and deer and boar and foxes and *tanuki*, the lumbering badger, could be seen and, rarely, the small brown bear. It would be a good eight days' march northeast of Nara before one reached the aborigines' country. Even there, unless a campaign was forward, there was seldom danger. If the escort were too small, a flight of arrows might whistle out of a thicket or a lagging porter be cut off from the rear of a troop. But no forces the enemy could muster would stand against the mounted knight or dared attack his spearmen. These original Ainu tribes used poison on their arrows, but their bows had short range compared to the splendid eight-foot war bow of the Japanese, with its pull of seventy pounds and its shaft, well over a cloth-yard length, tipped with iron and fletched with falcon.

The Ainu aborigines were by no means all unfriendly, and, when they were, it was in the furtive way of a conquered people. Often they were glad enough to supply the party with the fish and game they captured so adeptly. A greater danger came from such spirits of evil as might be abroad. These infested the spots where man failed to observe the proper rites or where his deliberate sin allowed them to congregate.

Most feared of all were the bands of well-armed robbers who had taken to the road. These were not aborigines, but Japanese outcasts, often well trained and desperate. Neither the villagers nor the local lord of the manor could always cope with them. They were mobile and would as soon attack the court messenger as a private traveler, provided they had a fair chance to beat down his resistance and despoil the party. The records of the time are crowded with rescripts, ordering suppression of the bandits by provincial levies and sending troops from the capital to guard the roads.

The lot of the plebeian in Nara at this time was indeed a hard one. His simple diet was, in good years, barely enough. He tasted little meat, especially in the city and communities dominated by nearby monasteries; but fish from river and sea have always been abundant in Japan. The capital, however, was far from the coast and has always been worse supplied with sea fish than any other considerable town. In the eighth century, during hot weather, ocean fish were never seen there except by the rich, who had it fetched across the hills from Naniwa (Ōsaka). But, then as now innumerable varieties were salted down to serve rather as relishes for cereals than for nourishment or bulk.

Rice was never staple for the lower classes. They steamed and boiled barley and millet, or made noodles and dumplings from their flour. During the two centuries before Nara city had been established, immigrants from Korea had been settled in the villages along the coast and over the great plain. These foreigners amalgamated with the Japanese and introduced their peculiar modes of pickling and fermenting greens, which, though never adopted by the Japanese in their full odoriferous richness of putrescence, brought new savories to the islands. Beans were a common small crop in the householder's garden patch, but *tōfu*, bean curd, was as yet a staple only of the monastic diet. On the whole, in spite of the total lack of butcher's meat, the peasant's diet, dull and unvaried as it was, seems to have been fairly nourishing. The sea fish, except on the Nara plain, and the various seaweeds of which he made good use, gave him iodine. What he conspicuously lacked was the animal fats.

His cooking flame was started by a fire drill of *hinoki* wood or by a flint. Charcoal from the communal kiln was his fuel when it could be afforded. But for many it was not procurable, and faggot gathering had already become a vital problem for the city poor, since the sacred groves were jealously guarded and the forest had receded far beyond the city limits. Cooking gear was unglazed pottery and perhaps a rare soapstone griddle or pot, such as is used today in Korea. Food was eaten off wood trenchers or out of shallow wood troughs and bowls and platted leaves.

Each family owned some sort of small pestle and mortar, but meal in larger quantities was usually ground at the communal millstone, turned by hand or by a cow, whose milk was never drunk nor her flesh eaten. Sometimes the nearest temple, as in China today, provided both threshing floor and millstone, where each family could take its turn at the grinding and leave a small portion in kind for tithes and rent.

The thatched cottages were dark in winter, earth floored and bitterly drafty. The clay stove was chimneyless; frequently all cooking was done, as in Europe, over an open pit lined with stones in the floor. In fact the whole dwelling was often a shallow pit, set round with stakes to support the rafters and thatch. Such huts were inundated during the rains and often consumed suddenly by fire. Beds were loose straw covered with a straw mat.

While courtiers and dignitaries of the church rode splashing by in splendid robes of brocade cut after the latest Chinese fashion, peasants went in breechclouts for seven months of the year, barefoot or straw sandaled. They thatched themselves, like their huts, with straw against snow or rain, and made rough capes and gowns from hemp twine or the string rolled from mulberry bark paper waterproofed with persimmon juice. The winter crowds clad in such fustian were somber enough. Their commonest dye was derived from the *tsuruba-me* tree that produced a dark brown color, so unfading that poets adopted this word to stand for unchanging love, in contrast to the more showy red that soon faded. The many priests were clad in cloth of reddish brown or dingy saffron, tinged by vegetable dyes. Only slaves seem to have worn undyed cloth, which, till white cotton became more usual, was a light tan color.

Animal hair and wool, banned by Buddhism, was totally lacking, except for the furs and the few felts brought from North China for court use. Cotton was now being grown in Kyushu but was not generally available. A wistful poem from the Manyo Shu (557–764) reflects the damp chill of the Japanese winter:

The wadded cloak looks warm.
I've never worn one.

Local floods, crop failures, or plagues that reduced the manpower of whole villages at a time, often left the peasant desperate. In such times of stress a community living in so hand-to-mouth a way suffered immediately. They starved to death. Only an occasional man or boy could escape to the frontiers or manage to enroll in the levies. These at least were fed and clothed by the government, though it is on record that no pay was available for the families of those up with the colors. To be tied to the land in time of famine or drought or plague was sentence of death. It is true that, in the middle of the seventh century, the good Prince Shōtoku had built several small reservoirs in the Asuka plain for impounding water against drought, and had installed granaries where stores were held against famine years. Buddhism and the prince's tender heart were to be thanked for that. But the practice was by no means general, nor was all he could do very far reaching. Government granaries existed at the capital and in the provinces, but these were nothing more than subtreasuries where taxes, paid in kind, were stored for the exclusive use of the government and carefully guarded against the poor.

So nurtured, and with such housing, the farmer or the city laborer went out to tend his field or ply his craft, while the wife and daughter tended cocoons to make the luxury silk they never flaunted. His crops and her silk were used for taxes. In such a hut they twisted the twine for nets and for their few garments; there they did their simple cooking.

The state of the laborer or peasant in the metropolitan district of Nara was much more advanced than that of his provincial cousin. Even when he devoted himself purely to farming, his son, by reason of the nearby monasteries and the court, had opportunities to learn a craft. Thus the lad helping with the balks of timber for the Daibutsu temple, if he proved himself handy at stripping bark and squaring trunks for the sawyers, could become a carpenter. His sister, helping at the nunnery, could graduate from unreeling cocoons and from spinning to become a weaver. But in the remoter countryside the chief crafts were those of the home, and the farmer's family practiced them all. The communal charcoal kilns were used by each household in turn, and the village pestle and mortar of stone or log in the same way. Also, as was once the case in parts of New England, the loom itself seems sometimes to have been common property—though it is not clear whether in Japan this was not the silk loom exclusively. Looms for the hemp and bark-string cloth were but the simplest frames, barely a foot wide.

If the upper classes got small book learning, farmers and laborers, from whom the artists sprang, got none. Their trades were taught them as apprentices, and their spiritual training consisted in the homely virtues of hard work and thrift and in Shinto observances. Europe before the Renaissance presents much the same picture of noble arts, produced for the church and court, contemporary with a great folk art of no less intrinsic beauty and perhaps even greater vitality and significance, all made, by means of a traditional and instinctive technique, by people who could count but not calculate and draw but not write.

The Extent of Japanese Borrowing from China

A major characteristic of this period of borrowing, as of those yet to come, is the way in which the Japanese adapted foreign patterns to fit their needs while retaining their own identity. Indeed, in the words of our next selection, Japan ". . . managed to retain unchanged its most fundamental institutions and beliefs." Nonetheless, it must be emphasized that China has had a powerful impact on the development of Japanese culture. Japanese have felt they had a special relationship with China from the days of Prince Shōtoku to the present when there is talk of Japan's "responsibility" to serve as a bridge between China and the rest of the world.

The nature and significance of Japan's relationship with China is analyzed in the following selection.

J. W. HALL AND R. K. BEARDSLEY,
Twelve Doors to Japan,
pp. 160–166

No society has been completely self-sufficient, and only a very few centers of distinctive civilization have arisen on this earth. It is more common to find peoples such as the Japanese or those of Western Europe whose cultures are compounded from many sources. . . .

The Japanese nation came of age in the Chinese zone of civilization, and a rehearsal of the interaction between Japanese and Chinese culture will help in our understanding of the country's later involvement with the West. The relationship between Japan and the more dominant Chinese cultural tradition which formed the wider environment surrounding the country in premodern times was far from that of simple and constant absorption by the Japanese. . . . On the one hand the pressure of Chinese influence was affected by the rise and fall of dynasties and by variations in China's cultural vitality, and on the other hand the absorptive capacity of the Japanese varied greatly according to circumstances within the country.

It should not be supposed that Japan was a particularly effective absorbent for Chinese culture. Many of the basic structural elements of Japanese society had been derived from a tradition quite different from that of the Chinese and had been set many centuries before Chinese influence touched Japan in any significant quantity. The political and social structure of the country during the *uji* [Yamato] period was more closely linked to the nomadic societies of Northeast Asia. The language was predominantly Altaic. As a consequence, China's first gifts to Japan were not the most easily assimilated. . . .

Moreover, despite many overlays of Chinese influence, Japanese culture managed to retain unchanged its most fundamental institutions and beliefs. Japan's seventh-century experiment in adopting Confucian-style government, for instance, never seriously attempted to destroy the aristocratic structure of Japanese society. Again, the tradition of a warrior aristocracy predominated over the attempt to create a conscript army on the Chinese model. The Japanese culture hero remained the military aristocrat, the samurai, not the Chinese type of literatus. The same persistence is noticeable with respect to certain ethical concepts governing the relationship of the individual to the family and to the state. Despite the strong emphasis upon family in Japan, loyalty to a political superior ideally outranked family loyalties. The Chinese ideal placed family loyalties first. Does this explain, perhaps, the ready acceptance of the feudal pattern of loyalties in Japan and the quick florescence of modern state patriotism? Certainly the "political man" in China and in Japan were differently motivated. Even in material culture, the Japanese showed many surprising areas of resistance to China: for instance, clothing, domestic architecture, and food.

Yet, having said all this, there is little doubt that Japanese culture, like that of Korea or Annam [in Southeast Asia], stands in the eyes of the comparative historian as simply a variant of the great East Asian tradition mothered by China. We have said that the Chinese impact on Japan was variable in terms of both intensity and quality. Matching the ebb and flow in Chinese influence was the cycle of Japan's own receptivity or lack thereof. The history of Chinese-Japanese cultural relations must be seen in terms of these variable factors.

Until the year 607 the Japanese people felt the influence of China mainly indirectly through the Korean Peninsula. . . . By the sixth century Japan had acquired some of the essentials of Chinese civilization: the writing system, the Confucian classics, the calendar, and crafts such as silk weaving and pottery making. Moreover, during the sixth century the introduction of Buddhism from Korea laid the foundation for a bridge of communication between the continent and Japan which was to prove of the greatest importance in the centuries to follow. Nonetheless, up to the seventh century Japanese culture remained fundamentally distinct from that of China in its political organization, social structure, and religious beliefs.

Beginning in the seventh century, several factors combined to bring Japan and China closer together. The many centuries of slow and indirect contact with the continent had laid a technological and intellectual base in Japan which now permitted the more rapid absorption of Chinese culture. Furthermore, conditions in Japan foreshadowed the breakdown of the Yamato social order and turned the interests of the Japanese elite to new techniques of government and religious organization. Meanwhile, China after several years of political disunity was being reunited by the Sui and T'ang emperors. From 607 to 838 the Japanese court sent twelve embassies to China in a conspicuous attempt to acquire the fruits of Chinese civilization. Social and political changes were intermixed with a flood of importations from China. . . .

Several features of the eighth-century Chinese influence upon Japan require comment. First, although Japan was seemingly engulfed by Chinese civilization at this time, a closer look will show that the Japanese were very much in control of what and how they borrowed from abroad. The political leaders appeared full of confidence in their ability to carry out internal reforms modeled after what they had learned, but not slavishly imitated, from China. . . . Second, it seems obvious that most histories have magnified the impact of China upon Japan because they have concentrated upon what transpired at the center of court activity and have neglected the rest of the country. Surely many areas were hardly touched by the influx of continental culture. Third, it is important to note that the Chinese civilization of the T'ang period was in many ways a rather special variant of the Chinese model. For instance, at no other time did Buddhism occupy so important a place in Chinese culture. Buddhism in fact colored the entire process of Japan's relations with China at this time (and later), for the Buddhist priesthood brought to Japan much more of the products of Chinese civilization than did even the official embassies of the period. Furthermore, after official relations lapsed, there were times when the only knowledge Japan received of China came through the reports of traveling priests. Thus the China which was exported to Japan was much more heavily colored by Buddhism than the ideal to which the Chinese subscribed. . . .

By the time the Fujiwara family had gained the upper hand at the court in Kyoto [mid-ninth century], a feeling of isolationism toward the continent had begun to set in. . . . From the ninth century, Japan and China drifted increasingly far apart. Yet during these years the Buddhist orders kept in touch with China, and it is to some extent the stimulus of what Japanese priests saw there that encouraged them to begin the propagation of the new Amida and Zen sects.

Japan's isolation from the continent was shattered by the Mongol invasions of 1274 and 1281. The dramatic repulse of these assaults by the warriors of the Kamakura shogunate proved a turning point in Japan's foreign relations. Heretofore the Japanese had depended almost entirely upon Chinese and Korean ships and crews to sail the East China Sea, but as part of the defense against the Mongols they had begun to build their own ships. With the disappearance of the Mongol threat, Japan revealed itself as an independent sea power. Japanese ships, largely freebooters known as *wakō*, began to rove the coasts of Korea and China.

From the time of the Mongol invasions, Japan's involvement in the affairs of the continent steadily increased. In 1342 the temple of Tenryūji began the practice of sending trading ships to China. Eventually, under the patronage of the Ashikaga shogunate, official trade relations were formalized between Japan and China, the Japanese accepting the role of tributary vassal to the Ming emperor. By this time, moreover, the nature of Japan's relations with China had changed. First of all, so-called "official relations" were conducted by the priests of certain Zen temples of Kyoto. Second, trade was now the all-important objective. Nor was such trade markedly one-sided, as it had once been. True enough, Japanese imports were mostly products of China's continued cultural superiority over Japan: copper coins, works of art, scholarly publications, medicines, and exotic stuffs. But the Japanese paid for such imports not only with raw copper, but also with their own manufactures, such as screens, fans, and peerless steel blades. Trade was becoming important for economic reasons. Japanese ports, such as Sakai, florished on the China trade, as did many of the provincial lords. There were cultural by-products of this trade, but these were largely apparent in the field of art. Japan remained feudal and Buddhist.

The sixteenth century was Japan's greatest period of overseas trade expansion prior to modern times. By now the Japanese were masters of the sea, and Japanese freebooters ranged the China Seas as far as Annam. *Daimyo* [feudal lords] vied for the opportunity to trade with the Portuguese or themselves fitted out vessels to send to the South Seas. But China was only indirectly involved in this activity. The Central Kingdom had by now declared the Japanese enemies of the empire. . . .

How surprising then that the Tokugawa period should witness a remarkable florescence of Chinese learning in Japan. Unlike the seventh-century chapter in Japan's emulation of China, the impetus behind the seventeenth-century flowering of neo-Confucianism was almost wholly a product of Japanese domestic needs and sprang not from any contemporaneous contact with China but rather from seeds already planted many centuries earlier. In the Japan newly unified under the Tokugawa house, shogun and *daimyō* both found in Confucianism the values for social and political order which they admired. Thus, while Buddhism went into a decline, Confucianism became the favored source of official morality and the basis of education. . . .

Yet left to their own devices the Japanese eventually outgrew their enthusiasm for Confucian scholarship. By the beginning of the nineteenth century Japan had almost totally lost touch with China. Trade at Nagasaki had nearly ceased. Chinese silks, which the Japanese had once sought so eagerly, were no longer in demand. The Japanese produced their own. In the intellectual field, new schools of thought challenged the supremacy of Confucianism. A newfound interest in Japan's own past called for the study of Japanese history and Shinto religious beliefs. Students of Western science had begun to attack the neo-Confucian cosmology. By the 1830s the Japanese had thoroughly absorbed Confucian ethics but had begun to grow restive under their subservience to Chinese culture. Once Japan's leaders acknowledged the superiority of Western culture, particularly science, the Japanese quickly abandoned their admiration for things Chinese. Within a few decades they could even pose as the superiors of the Chinese in adjusting themselves to the modern world. The Japanese invasion of China in the 1930s was frequently justified as an effort to "help" that country become a viable modern state.

Japan's relationship to China has not been that of constant emptyhanded borrowing. On the one hand China itself went through cycles of cultural brilliance and decline, and on the other hand Japan swung between extremes of eager emulation and outright hostility toward China. It is this interaction of differential impact and receptivity played out through a constant process of technological growth in Japan which has made for the complex pattern of Chinese influence upon the country. And while we may consider Chinese influence one of the major sources of change in Japanese history, we must bear in mind that the "Chinese impact" was itself affected by the evolution of Japan's own cultural institutions.

PART III. THE GROWTH OF NATIVE INSTITUTIONS (794-1185)

The Cult of Beauty

Toward the end of the eighth century the government decided to build a new capital, apparently to escape the influence of the great Buddhist monasteries headquartered in Nara. The new capital, Heian (later Kyoto), again followed the pattern of the contemporary Chinese capital, though this time on a larger scale than that employed at Nara.

Following the establishment of the new capital the era of wholesale adaptation of Chinese culture came gradually to an end. The power of the Chinese-style central government, never overwhelming in any case, declined as the great monasteries and powerful families managed to remove their estates from the tax roles.

One of the great families, the Fujiwaras, working from a power base of immense land holdings, was able in effect to take over the imperial court and rule the country through a vastly simplified governmental structure.

The estates of the nobility, scattered throughout the country, required the services of managers and warriors to operate and defend them. Though these rustics were looked down upon by their masters in the capital, they constituted the germ of feudalism, a system which was to dominate Japan from the thirteenth century to modern times.

However, it required several centuries for the warriors to develop and recognize their power, and during this time there occurred a great flowering of refined culture at the Fujiwara-dominated imperial court. As contacts with China drew to a halt, distinctively Japanese tastes came to the fore in the arts. Particularly noteworthy were the literary efforts of several ladies of the court who wrote in the newly devised phonetic symbols modified from Chinese characters to fit the needs of the completely unrelated Japanese language. The most famous of these is Lady Murasaki's *The Tale of Genji*—the world's first novel. This monumental work (still widely read in Japan) reveals in minute detail the refined tastes of the court aristocrats. The discovery, cultivation, and creation of beauty seem to have been the preoccupation of the courtiers—a process tinged, however, with sadness in the knowledge that beauty like life itself is transient.

The following selection, drawing heavily on *The Tale of Genji*, discusses the concern with aesthetic judgment which played so great a part in the lives of those at the court.

IVAN MORRIS
The World of the Shining Prince,
pp. 194–198

If [Lady] Murasaki's period did little for the intellectual progress of mankind, and still less for techniques of government and social organization, it will always be remembered for the way in which its people pursued that cult of beauty in art and in nature which has played so important a part in Japan's cultural history and which is perhaps the country's greatest contribution to the world. The 'rule of taste' applied not only to the formal arts but to nearly every aspect of the lives of the upper classes in the capital. It was central to Heian Buddhism, making (as Sir George Sansom has put it) religion into an art and art into a religion. In the conduct of a romantic liaison it prescribed not only how the lovers should write their poems and send their letters but the exact manner in which the man should get up in the morning and take his leave. The 'rampant aesthet-

icism' of the period extended even to the day-to-day
activities of the government, in which the officials were
expected to perform stylized dances as part of their
duties, and in which (as we know from a thirteenth-
century chronicle) the Intendant of the Imperial Police
was chosen for his good looks as much as for his family
connexions.

The immense leisure enjoyed by members of the
upper classes allowed them to indulge in a minute cultivation of taste. Their sophisticated aesthetic code applied even to the smallest details, such as the exact
shade of the blossom to which one attached a letter or
the precise nuance of scent that one should use for a
particular occasion. Taste in colour was developed to
a remarkable extent, and the literature of the time is
full of colour impressions, like those evoked by the
snow falling on a messenger's scarlet tunic or by a
gentleman's plum-coloured trousers seen against a background of dark green pines. The art of combining
colours was particularly important in men's and wom-
en's dress, and when a writer like Murasaki enters into
detail about the clothes that her characters are wearing
(detail that can become rather tiresome for the modern
reader) she is in fact telling us about their artistic
sensibility. The following passage from her diary suggests the importance that was attached to taste in
colour and the highly critical sense that had developed
by her time:

> The Empress was wearing the usual scarlet robe,
> under which she had kimonos of light plum, light
> green and yellow rose. His Majesty's outer robe
> was made of grape-coloured brocade; underneath
> he had a willow green kimono and, below that, one
> of pure white—all most unusual and up-to-date in
> both design and colour. . . . Lady Nakazukasa's
> robe, which was also of grape-coloured brocade,
> hung losely over a plain jacket of green and cherry.
> On that day all the ladies in attendance on His

Majesty had taken particular care with their dress. One of them, however, had made a small error in matching the colours at the openings of her sleeves. When she approached His Majesty to put something in order, the High Court Nobles and Senior Courtiers who were standing nearby noticed the mistake and stared at her. This was a source of lively regret to Lady Saishō and the others. It was not really such a serious lapse of taste; only the colour of one of her robes was a shade too pale at the opening.

Not only did the rule of taste extend to every sphere of life and apply to the smallest details, but (with the single exception of good birth) it took primacy over all else. Artistic sensibility was more highly valued than ethical goodness. Despite the influence of Buddhism, Heian society was on the whole governed by style rather than by any moral principles, and good looks tended to take the place of virtue. The word *yoki* ('good') referred primarily to birth, but it also applied to a person's beauty or to his aesthetic sensibility; the one implication it lacked was that of ethical rectitude. For all their talk about 'heart' and 'feeling', this stress on the cult of the beautiful, to the virtual exclusion of any concern with charity, sometimes lends a rather chilling impression to the people of Genji's world. *

Sensibility also preceded profundity, aesthetic experience invariably being more prized than abstract speculation. We have already noticed the general absence of interest in reasoning and in serious scholarship: erudite as they may be, the Confucian professors are regarded as absurd and unacceptable figures because they lack good, up-to-date taste. The overwhelming interest of the upper classes in the aesthetic side of life enabled Heian culture to make remarkable advances in certain directions, but kept it curiously backward in others.

---

* Prince Genji, the central figure in Murasaki's novel. [Ed.]

Finally, the aesthetic cult of the time provided the framework in which the 'good people' not only expressed but even experienced their emotions. Though emotional sensitivity was a mark of the true gentleman, it was kept within the limits of the accepted aesthetic code and rarely developed into wild passion or unrestrained romanticism. Even when Murasaki's characters are plunged into the most agonizing grief over the death of someone who has been close to them, they express their emotions in elegantly-turned poems of thirty-one syllables, whose central images of dew and dreams belong to the conventional aesthetic vocabulary.

The accepted pattern of sensibility that was so highly valued in Murasaki's time is summed up by *aware*, one of the many untranslatable (and relentlessly overworked) words that are used to define Japanese aesthetics. In its widest sense it was an interjection or adjective referring to the emotional quality inherent in objects, people, nature, and art, and by extension it applied to a person's internal response to emotional aspects of the external world. The gamut of its use in Heian literature is extremely wide. The word occurs over one thousand times in *The Tale of Genji* (one thousand and eighteen to be exact), and there has been many a learned disquisition on its different shades of meaning. Though in Murasaki's time *aware* still retained its early catholic range, its most characteristic use in *The Tale of Genji* is to suggest the pathos inherent in the beauty of the outer world, a beauty that is inexorably fated to disappear together with the observer. Buddhist doctrines about the evanescence of all living things naturally influenced this particular content of the word, but the stress in *aware* was always on direct emotional experience rather than on religious understanding. *Aware* never entirely lost its simple interjectional sense of 'Ah!'

Often the word appears in the phrase *mono no aware*, which roughly corresponds to *lacrimae rerum*, the pathos of things. It is when people perceive the connexion between the beauty and the sadness of the world that they most poignantly sense *mono no aware*. The sensitive observer is moved to tears by the beauty of nature, or by its embodiment in art (the Emperor's reaction to Genji's dance will be recalled), not only because it is so impressive in itself, but because when confronted with such beauty he becomes more than ever conscious of the ephemeral nature of all that lives in this world of ours. Scene after scene in *The Tale of Genji* reaches its emotional climax in this conjunction of aesthetic enjoyment with sorrow. Thus, when Genji visits the Cloistered Emperor Reizei at night, the gentlemen sit on the veranda nostalgically conversing about old times and about people who have long since died, while one of the courtiers plays the flute to the accompaniment of the bell-insects in the pine trees; the entire scene is suffused with moonlight and evokes an almost unbearable sense of *mono no aware*.

Yet, powerful though this feeling might become, it was, as we have seen, always circumscribed by a well-defined aesthetic code. Here was no turbulent, romantic emotion, lending itself to wild expressions of melancholy or grief. Rather it was a restrained and elegant form of sensibility, a quiet feeling of resignation that a well-bred man might experience when faced with the combination of the world's beauty and the ineluctable fate of all living things.

The ability to understand this type of aesthetic emotional experience (*mono no aware wo shiru*) was, of course, limited to the 'good people'. It was the equivalent of moral virtue in other societies, but it was a virtue that no member of the provincial or working classes could hope to acquire. Nor did it invariably accrue to people of good birth. Many a well-born character in contemporary literature is irretrievably damned by the comment that he or she does not 'know' *mono no aware*. Such people are 'bad', regardless of their birth, and regardless even of the conventional propriety of their behaviour. This category includes those who assume an understanding of *mono no aware* that they do not really feel. Such false sensibility emerged as a type of fashionable world-weariness which grew increasingly common in the later centuries as the expressions of *aware* became ever more conventionalized.

The cult of beauty helped to produce a society of great elegance and charm which, despite its many lacunae and its fatal weaknesses, will always occupy an important place in the world's cultural history. At a time when life in most of the West was unbelievably crude, it provided concepts of the refined life and of the complete gentleman that were not to reach Europe until the Renaissance. . . .

Language and Literature

The great developments in literature during the Heian period may justify the inclusion at this point of a discussion of the major characteristics of Japanese literature from its origins to the present. Important features of the language are also presented in the course of the following selection.

———————

DONALD KEENE,
Japanese Literature,
pp. 1–21

The question of the degree of Japan's indebtedness to China is so basic that I must discuss it briefly, before going on to any more critical consideration of the literature. It would be impossible to deny the enormous role played by China in the development of Japanese civilization. The method of writing, the philosophy, much of the religion, and certain literary genres had their origin in China, and Japanese have at all times professed the greatest admiration for the older culture, frequently paying it the supreme compliment of imitation. But if this is true of Japan's relationship to China it is equally true of France's and even England's to the classical world, although we do not say of Shakespeare's *Antony and Cleopatra* or of Racine's *Phèdre* that they are "nothing but" imitations. I do not think it fair, either, to say it about those Japanese works which obviously have their roots in China. With the exception of very short periods of indiscriminate borrowing, everything that Japan took from China was filtered through the basically different Japanese temperament and considerably modified. . . .

But Japan has been far more than a skilful modifier of Chinese civilization. In the field of literature, with which we are primarily concerned here, we shall find that Japanese poetry is in most ways unlike Chinese, that the Japanese were writing novels of magnitude and beauty centuries before the Chinese, and that the Japanese theater, far surpassing the Chinese, ranks with the great dramatic achievements of the world.

It is small wonder that Chinese and Japanese literature are so dissimilar, for the two languages are entirely different. Chinese is a monosyllabic language with musical tones to distinguish the many identical syllables. In its classical form at least, Chinese is a language of great compactness. Japanese, on the other hand, is polysyllabic, has no tones like the Chinese, and sounds rather like Italian, at least to those who do not know Italian. In contrast with the brevity of classical Chinese, Japanese is a language of interminable sentences—sometimes literally interminable, in which case they are left incomplete, at the end of the twentieth or fortieth subtle turn of phrase, as if their authors despaired of ever coming to the end of their task. Again, Chinese poetry is usually rhymed and is based on a complicated pattern of musical tones. In Japanese, on the other hand, rhyme is generally avoided, and the formal rules of prosody reduce themselves to a matter of counting syllables. Although the earliest Japanese poems we know, those preserved in a work of the early eighth century A.D., have lines of irregular length, the preference for alternating lines of five and seven syllables soon crystallized among Japanese poets, and this eventually became the basic rhythm of the language, found not only in poetry but in almost any type of literary composition.

To give an idea of the appearance of Japanese in transcription (with the consonants pronounced as in English, and the vowels as in Italian), I have chosen a passage, ostensibly in prose but in alternating lines of seven and five syllables. It is one of the most famous descriptions in the literature, the beginning of the lovers' suicide journey in the play *Love Suicides at Sonezaki,* written in 1703 by Chikamatsu. The young man and the young woman, believing that it is impossible for them to know happiness together in this life, set out in the early morning for the wood of Sonezaki, where they are to kill themselves.

Kono yo no nagori	Farewell to this world
Yo mo nagori	And to the night, farewell.
Shini ni yuku mi wo	We who walk the way to death
Tatōreba	To what should we be likened?
Adashi ga hara no	To the frost on the road
Michi no shimo	To the graveyard
Hitoashi zutsu ni	Vanishing with each
Kiete yuku	Step ahead:
Yume no yume koso	This dream of a dream
Aware nare	Is sorrowful.
Are kazōreba	Ah, did you count the bell?
Akatsuki no	Of the seven strokes
Nanatsu no toki ga	That mark the dawn
Mutsu narite	Six have sounded;
Nokoru hitotsu ga	The remaining one
Konjō no	Will be for this existence
Kane no hibiki no	The last echo
Kiki osame	We shall hear.
Jakumetsu iraku to	It will echo
Hibiku nari	The bliss of nothingness.

As one may easily see from the above, the sounds of Japanese are very simple. Each syllable generally consists of one consonant followed by one vowel. The restricted number of possible sounds has inevitably meant that there are many homonyms in the language, and countless words contain within themselves other words or parts of words of quite unrelated meanings. For example, the word *shiranami*, meaning "white waves", or the wake behind a boat, might suggest to a Japanese the word *shiranu*, meaning "unknown", or *namida* meaning "tears". Thus we have blending into one another three ideas, "unknown", "white waves", "tears". One can easily see how from a combination of such images a poem could grow—a boat sails for an unknown destination over the white waves, a lady watches the wake of her lover's boat in tears. From such a multiplicity of word associations evolved the *kakekotoba*, or "pivot-word", one of the most distinctive features of Japanese verse. The function of the "pivot-word" is to link two different images by shifting in its own meaning. This may be illustrated by the lines:

> What use are riches when you diamonds,
> Rubies and gold are dross.

In this crude example, "diamond" shifts as it is pronounced from the word "die", necessary to complete the thought "when you die" to the full meaning of the precious stone, as though the sound "die" started in the poet's subconscious mind a train of images associated with "riches".

The Japanese "pivot-word" shows a characteristic feature of the language, the compression of many images into a small space, usually by means of puns which expand the overtones of words. In English the use of the pun, or the play on words, for this purpose is not common, but there are examples even before Joyce pushed this method to the extreme with such creations as Meandertalltale. In *Macbeth*, for instance, at a highly tragic moment in the play occur the lines:

Your castle is surpriz'd; your wife and Babes
Savagely slaughtered: To relate the manner
Were on the Quarry of these murther'd Deere
To adde the death of you.

(IV, iii, 239–42.)

Shakespeare certainly did not intend the pun on "deer" and "dear" to be greeted with laughter; it serves rather to increase the complexity of the lines, as it would in a Japanese drama. The great number of similar-sounding words in Japanese affords a perhaps unique range of play on words. Puns were sometimes used for comic effects as in other languages, but the tragic pun was also developed, and it was even possible for poets to keep two different sets of images going at the same time through an entire poem without any awkwardness, as in this example:

> *Kie wabinu, utsurou hito no, aki no iro ni,*
> *mi wo kogarashi no, mori no shita tsuyu.*
> (SHIN KOKINSHŪ, 1205 A.D.)

One may give two almost entirely different translations of these lines. The first, the more personal interpretation, might be, "Sadly I long for death. My heart tormented to see how he, the inconstant one, is weary of me, I am weak as the forest dew." Or, by using other meanings of the sounds, "See how it melts away, that dew in the wind-swept forest, where the autumn colours are changing!" Neither of these translations is a full rendering, because in the poet's mind and words there is a constant shifting of the two sets of images, so that the dew which looks as if it soon must be melted away by the autumnal wind becomes one with the woman who has been abandoned by her bored lover, and who wonders what keeps her still alive. It is not that the dew is simply being used metaphorically to describe the woman's state (and to suggest her tears), for the image of the dew is used in its full sense of the natural phenomenon in the second rendering of the poem I gave. The author meant both to be understood at the same time, to draw as it were two concentric circles of meaning, each complete but indissolubly linked to the other.

The effect achieved in this poem was naturally possible only because of the variety of word-play that Japanese affords. But Japanese writers have always been sensitive to the overtones of words, and their exploitation of the possibilities of their language is not merely a fortuitous result of the ease of punning. . . .

It would be untrue to infer from this example, however, that all Japanese poetry is so extremely complicated in its expression. There are many relatively straightforward poems, and there has been more than one poet who has decried the artificiality of the poetry of his time and insisted on the virtues of simple sincerity. But simplicity and plain expression do not seem to be truly characteristic of the language, which is surely one of the world's vaguest yet most suggestive. Japanese sentences are apt to trail off into thin smoke, their whole meaning tinged with doubt by the use of little particles at the end, such as "perhaps", "may it not be so?"

The ambiguity in the language is such that at times, especially in the *Nō* plays, we may have the effect of listening to a string trio or quartet. There is a total melody which we can recognize, although we are at the same time aware that it is the combined product of the individual melodic lines of the several instruments. . . .

In Japanese literature the unexpressed is as carefully considered as the expressed, as in a Japanese painting the empty spaces are made to have as strong an evocative power as the carefully delineated mountains and pines. There always seems to be an instinctive reluctance to say the obvious words, whether they are "I am so happy" or "It is so sad". Seldom has it been desired to present the whole of any sight or experience. What the Japanese poets and painters were trying to do instead is perhaps best illustrated by a famous anecdote. It is related how one day a great general, clad in brilliantly polished armour, was waiting for an audience. He was informed that someone was coming who must not see him in armour, and he quickly threw about himself a thin gown of white silk. The effect of the polished armour glinting through the thin silk is the one at which the poets have aimed. To attempt to describe the full magnificence of the general in his armour, or the full beauty of a spring day, has not been the intent of Japanese writers. They have preferred to tell of the glint of the metal, or of the opening of a single blossom, and lead us thus to imagine the rest of the whole from which these few drops have been distilled.

The attempt to represent larger entities by small details resulted in a realism and concreteness in the images which contrast strangely with the misty ambiguity of the general effect. The splash of a frog jumping into the water, the shrill cries of the cicadas, the perfume of an unknown flower, may be the central image around which a Japanese poem is built. In this we may detect the influence of the philosophy of Zen Buddhism which taught, among other things, that enlightenment could come from any sudden perception. The splash of a frog disturbing the ancient stillness of a pond could be as valid a means of gaining enlightenment as any other, as well as the very embodiment of the movement of life.

It may be seen that the effect of suggesting a whole world by means of one sharp image is of necessity restricted to shorter verse forms, and it is in fact in such forms of expression that the Japanese have in general excelled. The literature contains some of the longest novels and plays in the world, some of them of high literary quality, but the special Japanese talent for exquisite and suggestive detail has not been matched by a talent for construction. The earliest novels, if so we may call them, were often little more than a number of poems and the circumstances which inspired them. Such unity as these books possessed came from the fact that all the poems were credited to one man, or to one Emperor's court, but no attempt was made to connect the amorous adventure which gave rise to one verse with the adventure on the following page. Even in the later novels there is no really sharp distinction between the world of poetry and the world of prose, probably because poetry played a more common role in Japanese society than it has ever played in ours. In *The Tale of Genji*, written about 1000 A.D., there are about 800 verses. Conversations often consist largely of poetry, and no lover would neglect to send a poem on the day after seeing his mistress. But however lovely these poems may be, it cannot be pretended that they are all essential to the plot of the novel. Most Japanese novels indeed tend to break up into almost entirely disconnected incidents in the manner of the old poetry-tales. In some of the novels there is at least the thread of historical fact to link the various ancedotes of disparate nature, but in other works we have digressions of no apparent relevance. Even in the modern Japanese novel, which has been much influenced by European examples, we find curiously lyrical sections floating like clouds over the rest of the work. For example, in *The Thin Snow** (*Sasame-yuki* 1946–9) by Tanizaki, the most important Japanese novel published in the years following the war, there is an exquisite scene in which several of the principal characters go hunting fireflies of a summer night. Remembering from old novels and poetry the descriptions of elegant court ladies in long-sleeved kimonos catching the fireflies in silken nets, they at first feel disappointed, for they see before them only a muddy ditch in the open fields. But gradually, as the insects fill the air with glowing points of light, they are captured by the beauty so long familiar to them in poetry, and the description rises to lyrical heights worthy of *The Tale of Genji*.

---

* English translation titled: *The Makioka Sisters*. [Ed.]

If this incident does not advance very greatly the plot of *The Thin Snow*, nor give us any better understanding of the characters, it is beautiful in itself, and serves in an indefinite but real way to give us an impression of life in the Japan of 1939, just as the poetry in *The Tale of Genji* recreates for us the Japan of 950 years before. The digressions in Japanese novels may betray a weakness in the novelists' powers of construction, but often their intrinsic beauty is such that our enjoyment of the whole work is not lessened by the disunity. In retrospect it is as brilliantly coloured bits somehow merging into an indefinite whole that we remember the novel. And, as the European impressionist painters create an illusion of reality in spite of the fact that their landscapes are composed of seemingly arbitrary splashes of green, orange, blue, and all the other colours, so the apparently disconnected incidents of a Japanese novel, blending into one another, leave us with an imprecise understanding of their life.

Certain genres of literature have developed to a greater extent in Japan than in other countries, perhaps as a result of the difficulty experienced by Japanese writers in organizing their lyrical impressions and perceptions. These are the diary, the travel account, and the book of random thoughts, works which are relatively formless, although certainly not artless. The charm and refinement of such works may be illustrated by one of the travel accounts, *The Narrow Road of Oku*, by the seventeenth-century poet Bashō. This work begins:

The months and days are the travellers of eternity. The years that come and go are also voyagers. Those who float away their lives on boats or who grow old leading horses are forever journeying, and their home is wherever their travels take them. Many of the men of old died on the road, and I too for years past have been stirred by the sight of a solitary cloud drifting with the wind to ceaseless thoughts of roaming.

Last year I spent wandering along the seacoast. In autumn I returned to my cottage on the river and swept away the cobwebs. At last the year drew to its close. When spring came and there was mist in the air, I thought of crossing the barrier of Shirakawa into Oku. Everything I saw suggested travel, and I was so possessed by the gods that there was no controlling my mind. The spirits of the road beckoned, and I found I could do no work at all.

I patched up my torn trousers and changed the cords on my bamboo hat. To strengthen my legs for the journey I had moxa burned on my shins. Then the thought of the moon at Matsushima began to occupy my thoughts. When I sold my cottage and moved to Sampū's villa, to stay there until I started on my journey, I hung this poem on a post in my hut.

Kusa no to mo	Even a thatched hut
Sumikawaru yo zo	In this changing world may turn
Hina no ie	Into a doll's house.

When I set out on the 27th March, the dawn sky was misty. Though the pale morning moon had lost its light, Fuji could still be seen faintly. The cherry blossoms on the boughs at Ueno and Yanaka stirred sad thoughts within me, as I wondered when, if ever, I should see them again. My dearest friends had all come to Sampū's house the night before so that they might accompany me on the boat part of the way that morning. When we disembarked at a place called Senju, the thought of parting for so long a journey filled me with sadness. As I stood on the road that was perhaps to separate us forever in this dreamlike existence, I wept tears of farewell.

Yuku haru ya	Spring soon ends—
Tori naki uo no	Birds will weep, while in
Me wa namida	The eyes of fish are tears.

In such works the Japanese have been happiest, able as they are in them to give us their inimitable descriptions of nature, and their delicate emotional responses, without the necessity of a formal plot. A gentle humour and a gentle melancholy fill these pages. This desire to blend images into images, found throughout Japanese poetry, here takes the form of diverse experiences, whether the adventures of a journey, or the day-to-day happenings at the court, blended into the personality of the narrator. There is a general smoothing away of the rough edges of emotion, as something indecorous and rather vulgar. Much is sadly evocative, very little is shattering, either in these books of personal reflections or elsewhere in Japanese literature. Even in the direct imitations by Japanese poets and artists of foreign works, there is always a disinclination to lose the native lightness and grace. The heart-breaking grief experienced by a Chinese poet on seeing the destruction of his city will find its echo in the sweetly nostalgic recollections of his Japanese imitator. Or the portrait of a Taoist immortal, filled by the Chinese artist with an intense sense of mystery, becomes, in an almost direct Japanese copy, a charming composition of the immortal, his magic toad, pine-trees and clouds. . . .

The virtuoso approach to literature, and to art as well, where the artist attempts to do essentially the same thing as his predecessors but in a slightly different way, is characteristic of Japan. The technique may be illustrated most clearly by the following examples. The first is a *haiku* by Buson (1716–84):

Tsurigane ni	On the temple bell
Tomarite nemuru	Resting, asleep
Kochō ka na	A butterfly.

The second example is by Shiki (1867–1902):

Tsurigane ni	On the temple bell
Tomarite hikaru	Resting, glowing
Hotaru ka na	A firefly.

There is no question here of plagiarism; rather, Shiki assumed that the persons reading his *haiku* would be familiar with Buson's, and undoubtedly hoped that the new touches which his sensibility imposed on the old poem would be welcomed by a discriminating audience. Objectively viewed, Shiki's *haiku* is as good as Buson's, although a Western reader would condemn Shiki's as derivative, and his first impulse might be to write a parody of his own such as . . . "On the temple bell, Resting, chirping, A grasshopper."

Previous to the Meiji Restoration [1868] there had existed a great gap between the colloquial and literary languages. Even the writers of popular romances had used a modified form of the older literary language with its distinctive grammar and vocabulary. But with the large-scale translation of works from English and other European languages it became necessary to make increasing use of the colloquial language in literary expressions, for it was found hopelessly awkward to render the conversational approach of the English novel into the flowery patterns of literary-Japanese. The new colloquial style was used not only in translations, but in all works which had been influenced by European example.

There were, it is true, violent protests from various quarters against the adulation accorded to European examples, but although successful in some political and religious matters, such protests failed in so far as literature was concerned. In the past seventy years or more Japanese literature has been intimately affected by all European trends and, in fact, may be regarded in effect as forming a part of the modern movement in Western literature. . . .

The influence of the West was probably less marked on Japanese poetry than any other branch of literature. Many of the novelists of the new school had already gained fame as translators before publishing their own works, and they reveal at every moment their indebtedness to Western writers, even when the subject is purely Japanese. . . . Even the few novelists who have deliberately affected the old style betray in a thousand ways how much closer they are to the Western novel than to the traditional Japanese one. But the poets have not been so ready to abandon the old forms. Although new styles of poetry were evolved at about the same time for poetry as for the novel and for drama, the best poets continued for the most part to write in the traditional forms, and even works in the new style were likely to fall into the conventional pattern of alternating lines of five and seven syllables, the basic rhythm of the language. The decision of the poets to retain the traditional forms may show that there is a greater conservatism in poetry than in any other genre of literature, or it may represent an awareness that the brief poems were after all the most suited to the language, and more capable of achieving the impressionistic effects sought by the modern poets than the formless free verse. Certainly no modern poet has managed to suggest more with so few words than did Issa (1763–1828) after the death of his only surviving child. We may imagine that his friends attempted to console him with the usual remarks on the evanescence of the things of this world, and the meaninglessness of this existence as compared to the eternal life in Buddha's Western Paradise. Issa wrote:

Tsuyu no yo wa	The world of dew
Tsuyu no yo nagara	Is a world of dew and yet,
Sarinagara	And yet.

PART IV. THE FEUDAL AGE (1185–1868)

The Evolution of Feudalism

The warrior class which had been growing in power during the later Heian period moved to the center of the political stage in the twelfth century when power struggles among various factions in the capital resulted in calls to the provinces for military aid. The resulting conflict between the Minamoto (or Genji) and Taira (or Heike) warrior cliques continued sporadically for nearly fifty years until the Minamoto emerged victorious and established a new form of military government at the isolated fishing village of Kamakura (near present Tokyo) in 1185. The struggle between the Minamoto and the Taira has been such a favored theme in Japanese literature that, even today, one can count on seeing some part of the saga (considerably embellished) on stage or screen at some point in the year.

The feudal era, especially the Tokugawa regime (1600–1868), is of particular importance since it constituted the foundation from which Japan launched into its spectacularly successful modernization.

Readers familiar with European feudalism will notice many similarities with the Japanese system. They must not, however, equate feudalism with political disunity as they might be tempted to do on the basis of the European pattern. Japan, as we shall see, experienced both disunity and unity as its feudal structure evolved.

The evolution of Japanese feudalism can be divided into three phases. During the first phase (Kamakura period, 1185–1333), the warrior class (bushi or samurai), who had evolved during the Heian period as the administrators and protectors of the estates, destroyed Fujiwara power and established effective political control over Japan. This was accomplished through a network of personal loyalties focused upon the shogun (military dictator), who in turn was nominally the agent of the emperor in Kyoto.

The second stage (Muromachi period, 1333–1568) was marked by the disintegration of the shogun's effective control and the rise of independent feudal domains (hans) governed by powerful local lords (daimyos). Thus, the Europeans found on their arrival in the mid-sixteenth century a society similar in many respects to that of feudal Europe. Peasants functioned as serfs under the direction of knights (samurai) who in turn owed complete loyalty to their lords (daimyos). Commerce was actively carried on both within and far beyond the boundaries of Japan, most of it under the control of various daimyos and Buddhist sects. Many Buddhist sects possessed extensive land holdings and military forces, while others (notably the Zen sects) contributed directly to a flourishing of the arts.

The third phase (Momoyama period, 1568–1600; Tokugawa period, 1600–1868) witnessed the growth of a central government powerful enough to dominate the daimyos but not to eliminate them. The major role in this process of unification was played by Hideyoshi, a military genius of peasant birth, who enjoyed a brief near-dictatorial rule until his death in 1598. One of Hideyoshi's major vassals, Iyeyasu Tokugawa was able after a brief struggle with several rivals to gain control and to further consolidate the power of the central government.

The following selection discusses the emergence of this remarkable centralized phase of Japanese feudalism while noting the impact of the Europeans whose arrival may well have accelerated the process.

EDWIN O. REISCHAUER AND J. K. FAIRBANK,
East Asia, pp. 579–583

By the middle of the sixteenth century, Japanese feudalism showed many of the same signs of breakdown that had appeared in European feudalism as it gave way to the more centralized monarchies of early modern times. This disintegration could be seen in the expansion of domestic and foreign trade, the rise of commercial towns, the breakdown of the old class structure as the functional distinction between warrior-aristocrats and commoners became blurred, and the appearance of religious and commercial groupings of commoners who could challenge the military power and political authority of the feudal lords. Most important, the feudal privileges and autonomous status of vassals, rear vassals and the lesser feudal elements had begun to be submerged by the growing absolutism of the stronger daimyo.

By analogy with the European experience, it might seem that Japanese feudalism was about to be supplanted entirely by one or more unified "kingdoms" comparable to those of early modern Europe. Indeed, the overseas expansion of Europe at this time did have its counterpart in the great activities of the Japanese traders in the sixteenth century. But the political reunification of the islands followed a very different course from that taken by the rising national states of Europe. Japan underwent no radical reshaping of political and social institutions such as Europe experienced in the eventual end of feudalism, the Reformation and the Counter-Reformation, and the rise of mercantilism. The Japanese found a simpler, less revolutionary solution to the problems posed by new stimuli from abroad and the need to bring effective unity to a feudal society. They built upon the older feudal order, instead of sweeping it away, and they eliminated most of the foreign stimuli, instead of continuing their overseas commercial expansion.

Thus Japan, rather than developing into a modern national state in commercial and military competition with the other countries of the world, entered into the third major phase of its feudal development—a phase characterized by political unity and national isolation.

The country was reunified and subjected to a central political control that proved in some ways as thorough and efficient as that of any European state before the age of Napoleon, but the basic patterns of social organization and political structure remained entirely feudal. Any comparable stage in European feudalism—if such a stage ever existed—must have been very transitory. In fact, according to European notions the efficiently controlled system of late Japanese feudalism seems almost a contradiction in terms.

By choosing a simple, evolutionary solution to their problems in the sixteenth and early seventeenth centuries, the Japanese were able to attain effective unity and stability much more rapidly than the new national states of Europe. The stability they achieved, however, though an immediate blessing, may have been in the end a calamity for them, because it completely inhibited further development of economic, political and social institutions. During the next two centuries Japan's institutional and technological progress certainly did not keep pace with that of the West. As a result, the social and political order that took shape in Japan about the time of the first settling of the American colonies maintained its essential structure for more than two centuries, until the new nation that evolved from the small American colonies had expanded across a whole continent and, reaching across the broad Pacific, became a prime agent in the ultimate downfall of Japan's late feudal order. Institutional and technological backwardness in comparison with the West—this was the price the Japanese had to pay in the nineteenth century for the peace and political stability their ancestors had been enjoying for many generations.

It is not easy to explain why Japan, whose feudal development had paralleled Europe's in so many ways, took such a different historical turn during the sixteenth century. One reason may have been that feudal Japan maintained stronger traditions of political unity than those of the emerging states of feudal Europe, and therefore effective unity could be created without great revolutionary changes. The clarity of the geographical unit and the strong awareness of a long period of unified government throughout Japan contrasted with the vagueness of many national boundaries in Europe and with the tradition of a universal, polyglot Roman Empire, rather than a single clear-cut state. Because of these differences, the achievement of effective national units had been a much more difficult process in Europe, requiring the destruction of feudalism itself, while in Japan a united state could be achieved simply by building with the elements provided by the feudal system.

Another reason was certainly the greater distance of Japan from rival powers. A great increase in contact with the outside world during the sixteenth century seems to have contributed to the rapid reunification of Japan, but the protective seas and the remoteness of the country permitted the Japanese, when they became fearful of foreign influences at the beginning of the seventeenth century, to reimpose a considerable degree of isolation. Behind this artificially erected barrier, they were spared the sharp military and economic competition that impelled each of the rival states of Europe to forge ahead institutionally and technologically. Once unity had been achieved, the Japanese were able to put a sharp brake even to evolutionary change. They could thus maintain what seems by Western standards an anachronistic survival of feudal institutions within a society which in technology, economic development and effective political controls compared respectably with the most advanced of the European monarchies of the early seventeenth century.

While the reunification of Japan resulted mainly from the long process of domestic evolution, the sudden appearance of European traders and missionaries in the sixteenth century was undoubtedly a contributory factor. The military and naval skills of the European powers and the teachings of European missionaries posed a definite threat to Japan that called for a unified response. Moreover, the weapons and possibly other of the technological advances introduced by the Europeans facilitated the necessary centralization of power.

Soon after the Portuguese found their way around Africa and then pushed on to India in 1498, they and other European explorers began to dominate the great maritime trade routes that had existed for some seven or eight centuries along the coasts of Asia. The Portuguese reached Japan only a half century after they rounded the Cape of Good Hope. The first group to arrive landed at Tanegashima, an island off the southern tip of Kyūshū, apparently in 1543. Within a few years, Portuguese vessels were frequenting the ports of Kyūshū. In 1549 the Jesuit missionary Francis Xavier started preaching Christianity in West Japan and also in Kyōto.

Although the Portuguese seem to have had a certain contempt for the other Asians they had met, they respected and liked the Japanese. Evidently they were attracted by the martial skills and strong sense of honor of the feudal warrior class—qualities the Europeans could understand and appreciate because of their own feudal background. The Japanese similarly respected the Jesuit missionaries as men of discipline and learning, comparable to their own Zen priests. In fact, Christianity at first appeared to them as only another variant of the Buddhist doctrines that were so popular in Japan. Both sides too were eager for the profits of trade, and the Japanese, with their old realization that much could be learned from abroad, were receptive to both the religion and the material civilization of the Portuguese.

The daimyo of Kyūshū, who wished to entice the lucrative Portuguese trade to their respective ports, often showered favors on the missionaries, because of the missionaries' influence over their lay compatriots. Some daimyo, motivated more by a desire for economic profit than for spiritual gain, embraced Christianity and forced the people in their realms to follow suit. The small Ōmura daimyo became a Christian as early as 1562. In 1571 he established his town of Nagasaki as the chief port of call for the Portuguese ships and in 1579 he gave the government of this rapidly rising community to the Jesuits. The much greater Ōtomo daimyo was baptized in 1578.

The religious intolerance of the missionaries soon stirred up strong opposition among the Buddhist clergy, who in turn often induced the local political authorities to expel the missionaries or proscribe their religion. Many of those who had become converts for economic reasons, or who had been forced to do so by their lords, later abandoned the faith. There were, however, many sincere believers. Those in the capital district, where trade did not figure among the inducements, were particularly earnest, although the faith remained numerically strongest in Kyūshū.

The Christians in Japan have been estimated to have numbered 150,000 around 1582, about 300,000 by the end of the century, and perhaps as many as 500,000 in 1615. They thus constituted a much larger proportion of the population than they do today. In fact, Japan was the Jesuits' most promising missionary field in Asia. Wholly aside from forced conversions and economic inducements, Christianity seems to have met a greater response in Japan than in neighboring lands. It is hard to say why this was so, but the relative receptivity of the Japanese to foreign influences, the resemblance of certain aspects of Christianity to Japanese Buddhism, the similarity of Japanese feudal ideals to those of Europe, and the mutual respect of the Japanese and Portuguese must all have been factors.

The trade with the Portuguese and the technological advances they introduced probably had a more immediate effect on Japanese society and government than did Christianity. The coming of the large Portuguese ships had meant a further expansion of foreign trade, which in turn stimulated general economic growth and thus helped intensify the conditions that were leading to the breakdown of the old feudal system. New plants, such as tobacco and potatoes from the Americas, were introduced and in time considerably affected agriculture. The Japanese were much interested in the mechanical wares of the Europeans and found the Portuguese themselves fascinating. There was a veritable craze for everything Portuguese. At times modish Japanese even adopted European dress. Many Portuguese words entered the language, and a few, such as *pan* for "bread," still survive. A number of decorative painted screens of the period accurately portray the Portuguese ships and traders and the tall, forbidding missionaries. Since the Portuguese had arrived in Japan from the south and appeared to the Japanese to be dark-complexioned southerners, these paintings were called "Screens of the Southern Barbarians" (Namban-byōbu).

With their strong military concern, the Japanese were particularly interested in the firearms and the techniques of warfare that the Portuguese brought with them from Europe. In fact, they were so impressed by the arquebuses [firearms] of the first Portuguese who reached Tanegashima in 1543 that for a long time all firearms went by the name of *tanegashima*. Within a couple of decades of their introduction, guns had become a major weapon in Japanese warfare.

The Europeans may also have introduced improved methods of castle construction. In any case, the century following the arrival of the Portuguese was the greatest period of castle building in Japanese history, and all of Japan's existing castles date from that time. These castles had wide moats and massive earth-backed stone walls that could easily withstand the cannon-fire of the day, but the buildings themselves were flimsy by comparison with European castles, being made of thick, whitewashed mud walls on wooden frameworks.

All this had immediate military repercussions. The

richer daimyo, who could afford the new weapons and build the new type of fortress, became all the more dominant over their poorer and less modernized rivals. Thus they employed European innovations to accelerate the centralization of military and political power, which had already been started partly because of the threat posed by the Europeans' arrival.

The Tokugawa Military Code

The Tokugawa government, like all the military governments since the twelfth century, was the agent of the emperors in Kyoto. But, in fact, the court continued to be powerless and virtually inaccessible. The organizational genius of Iyeyasu Tokugawa (something of a hero to modern Japanese businessmen) produced a military government of such effectiveness that it has been referred to as the closest approximation to a totalitarian system ever to appear in a preindustrial society. The Tokugawa regime provided Japan with more than two centuries of internal peace and stability; but the price was high. Contacts with Westerners were deemed an unstabilizing factor; so the country became a "hermit nation." Japanese were forbidden on pain of death to leave their own shores. Christianity, too, was judged to be a danger, and a program of systematic persecution culminating in a major battle led to the deaths of perhaps as many as thirty thousand native Christians and the elimination of the religion in all but a few isolated mountain villages.

Each of the four classes into which the society was arbitrarily frozen—samurai, farmer, artisan, and merchant—was burdened with detailed and harshly enforced regulations. The government went to particular pains to prevent an alliance of any disgruntled daimyos. One of the many regulations required that either the daimyo or his immediate family must be in residence at the Tokugawa headquarters (Edo: now Tokyo) at all times. Checkpoints were established at intervals along all major highways to ensure that travelers carried the necessary passports. Even the design of clothing for the various classes was prescribed by law.

The following excerpts from the laws governing the military class serve to illustrate the nature of Tokugawa rule.

Text from RYUSAKU TSUNODA et al., eds.,
Sources of Japanese Tradition,
I, 326–329

[1] The arts of peace and war, including archery and horsemanship, should be pursued single-mindedly.

From of old the rule has been to practice "the arts of peace on the left hand, and the arts of war on the right"; both must be mastered. Archery and horsemanship are indispensable to military men. Though arms are called instruments of evil, there are times when they must be resorted to. In peacetime we should not be oblivious to the danger of war. Should we not, then, prepare ourselves for it?

[2] Drinking parties and wanton revelry should be avoided.

In the codes that have come down to us this kind of dissipation has been severely proscribed. Sexual indulgence and habitual gambling lead to the downfall of a state.

[3] Offenders against the law should not be harbored or hidden in any domain.

Law is the basis of social order. Reason may be violated in the name of the law, but law may not be violated in the name of reason. Those who break the law deserve heavy punishment.

[4] Great lords (daimyō), the lesser lords, and officials should immediately expel from their domains any among their retainers or henchmen who have been charged with treason or murder.

Wild and wicked men may become weapons for overturning the state and destroying the people. How can they be allowed to go free?

[5] Henceforth no outsider, none but the inhabitants of a particular domain, shall be permitted to reside in that domain.

Each domain has its own ways. If a man discloses the secrets of one's own country to another domain or if the secrets of the other domain are disclosed to one's own, that will sow the seeds of deceit and sycophancy.

[6] Whenever it is intended to make repairs on a castle of one of the feudal domains, the [shogunate] authorities should be notified. The construction of any new castles is to be halted and stringently prohibited.

"Big castles are a danger to the state." Walls and moats are the cause of great disorders.

[7] Immediate report should be made of innovations which are being planned or of factional conspiracies being formed in neighboring domains.

"Men all incline toward partisanship; few are wise and impartial. There are some who refuse to obey their masters, and others who feud with their neighbors." Why, instead of abiding by the established order, do they wantonly embark upon new schemes?

[8] Do not enter into marriage privately [i.e., without notifying the shogunate authorities]. . . . To form an alliance by marriage is the root of treason.

[9] Visits of the *daimyō* to the capital are to be in accordance with regulations.

The *Chronicles of Japan, Continued*, contains a regulation that "Clansmen should not gather together whenever they please, but only when they have to conduct some public business; and also that the number of horsemen serving as an escort in the capital should be limited to twenty. . . ." Daimyō should not be accompanied by a large number of soldiers. Twenty horsemen shall be the maximum escort for daimyō with an income of from one million to two hundred thousand *koku* of rice. For those with an income of one hundred thousand *koku* or less, the escort should be proportionate to their income. On official missions, however, they may be accompanied by an escort proportionate to their rank.

[10] Restrictions on the type and quality of dress to be worn should not be transgressed.

Lord and vassal, superior and inferior, should observe what is proper to their station in life. [Then follows an injunction against the wearing of fine white damask or purple silk by retainers without authorization.]

[11] Persons without rank shall not ride in palanquins [enclosed sedan chairs].

From of old there have been certain families entitled to ride in palanquins without special permission, and others who have received such permission. Recently, however, even the ordinary retainers and henchmen of some families have taken to riding about in palanquins, which is truly the worst sort of presumption. Henceforth permission shall be granted only to the lords of the various domains, their close relatives and ranking officials, medical men and astrologers, those over sixty years of age, and those ill or infirm. In the cases of ordinary household retainers or henchmen who willfully ride in palanquins, their masters shall be held accountable.

Exceptions to this law are the court families, Buddhist prelates, and the clergy in general.

[12] The samurai of the various domains shall lead a frugal and simple life.

When the rich make a display of their wealth, the poor are humiliated and envious. Nothing engenders corruption so much as this, and therefore it must be strictly curbed.

[13] The lords of the domains should select officials with a capacity for public administration.

Good government depends on getting the right men. Due attention should be given to their merits and faults; rewards and punishments must be properly meted out.

If a domain has able men, it flourishes; if it lacks able men it is doomed to perish. This is the clear admonition of the wise men of old.

The purport of the foregoing should be conscientiously observed.

A Merchant of Kyoto

Though Tokugawa policy was based on the concept of an agricultural society, there was, in fact, substantial growth in commerce and manufacturing. The government unintentionally fostered this expansion through the creation of great administrative centers such as Edo (now Tokyo) which had a population of one million by 1800. This "feudal" city was probably the largest in the world, as it is today.

With the growth in numbers and influence of the townsmen came new cultural forms designed to meet their worldly tastes. These included new forms of theater, woodblock printing (mostly of beautiful women), and a prose literature far removed in content and style from that admired by the samurai or the court nobility. The following tale by Ihara Saikaku (1642–1693), one of the most popular writers of the era, provides a tongue-in-cheek description of a highly successful merchant of Kyoto.

Text, by Saikaku Ihara, from
DONALD KEENE, ed.,
Anthology of Japanese Literature,
pp. 357–362

"This is to certify that the person named Fuji-ichi, tenant in a house belonging to Hishiya Chozaemon, is to my certain knowledge the possessor of one thousand *kamme* in silver. . . ."

Such would be the form of testimonial when Fuji-ichi sought new lodgings. It was his proud claim that in the whole wide world there was no millionaire quite like himself. For although he was worth a thousand *kamme*, he lived in a rented house no more than four yards wide. In this way he became the talk of Kyoto. However, one day he accepted a house as surety for a loan of thirty-eight *kamme*; in the course of time, as the interest mounted, the surety itself became forfeit; and for the first time Fuji-ichi became a property owner. He was much vexed at this. Up to now he had achieved distinction as "the millionaire in lodgings," but now that he had a house of his own he was commonplace— his money in itself was mere dust by comparison with what lay in the strong rooms of the foremost merchants of Kyoto.

Fuji-ichi was a clever man, and his substantial fortune was amassed in his own lifetime. But first and foremost he was a man who knew his own mind, and this was the basis of his success. In addition to carrying on his regular business, he kept a separate ledger, bound from odd scraps of paper, in which, as he sat all day in his shop, pen in hand, he entered a variety of chance information. As the clerks from the money exchanges passed by he noted down the market ratio of copper and gold; he inquired about the current quotations of the rice brokers; he sought information from druggists' and haberdashers' assistants on the state of the market at Nagasaki; for the latest news on the prices of ginned cotton, salt, and saké, he noted the various days on which the Kyoto dealers received dispatches from the Edo branch shops. Every day a thousand things were entered in his book, and people came to Fuji-ichi if they were ever in doubt. He became a valuable asset to the citizens of Kyoto.

Invariably his dress consisted of an unlined vest next to his skin, and on top of that a cotton kimono, stuffed on occasion with three times the usual amount of padding. He never put on more than one layer of kimono. It was he who first started the wearing of detachable cuffs on the sleeves—a device which was both fashionable and economical. His socks were of deerskin and his clogs were fitted with high leather soles, but even so he was careful not to walk too quickly along the hard main roads. Throughout life his only silk garments were of pongee, dyed plain dark blue. There was one it is true, which he had dyed a persistently undisguisable seaweed brown, but this was a youthful error of judgment, and he was to regret it for the next twenty years. For his ceremonial dress he had no settled crests, being content with a three-barred circle or a small conventional whirl, but even during the summer airing time he was careful to keep them from direct contact with the floor. His pantaloons were of hemp, and his starched jacket of an even tougher variety of the same cloth, so that they remained correctly creased no matter how many times he wore them.

When there was a funeral procession which his whole ward was obliged to join, he followed it perforce to the cemetery, but coming back he hung behind the others and, on the path across the moor at Rokuhara, he and his apprentices pulled up sour herbs by the roots.

"Dried in the shade," he explained, "they make excellent stomach medicine."

He never passed by anything which might be of use. Even if he stumbled he used the opportunity to pick up stones for fire-lighters, and tucked them in his sleeve. The head of a household, if he is to keep the smoke rising steadily from his kitchen, must pay attention to a thousand things like this.

Fuji-ichi was not a miser by nature. It was merely his ambition to serve as a model for others in the management of everyday affairs. Even in the days before he made his money he never had the New Year rice cakes prepared in his own lodgings. He considered that to bother over the various utensils, and to hire a man to pound the rice, was too much trouble at such a busy time of the year; so he placed an order with the rice-cake dealer in front of the Great Buddha. However, with his intuitive grasp of good business, he insisted on paying by weight—so much per pound. Early one morning, two days before the New Year, a porter from the cake-maker, hurrying about his rounds, arrived before Fuji-ichi's shop and, setting down his load, shouted for someone to receive the order. The newly pounded cakes, invitingly arrayed, were as fresh and warm as spring itself. The master, pretending not to hear, continued his calculations on the abacus, and the cake-man, who begrudged every moment at this busy time of the year, shouted again and again. At length a young clerk, anxious to demonstrate his businesslike approach, checked the weight of the cakes on the large scales with a show of great precision, and sent the man away.

About two hours later Fuji-ichi said: "Has anyone taken in the cakes which arrived just now?"

"The man gave them to me and left long ago," said the clerk.

"Useless fellow!" cried Fuji-ichi. "I expect people in my service to have more sense! Don't you realize that you took them in before they had cooled off?"

He weighed them again, and to everyone's astonishment their weight had decreased. Not one of the cakes had been eaten, and the clerk stood gazing at them in open-mouthed amazement.

It was the early summer of the following year. The local people from the neighborhood of the Eastern Temple had gathered the first crop of eggplants in wicker baskets and brought them to town for sale. "Eat young eggplants and live seventy-five days longer" goes the saying, and they are very popular. The price was fixed at two coppers for one eggplant, or three coppers for two, which meant that everybody bought two.

But Fuji-ichi bought only one, at two coppers, because—as he said—"With the one copper I now have in pocket I can buy any number of larger ones when the crop is fully grown."

That was the way he kept his wits about him, and he seldom made a mistake.

In an empty space in his grounds he planted an assortment of useful trees and flowers such as willow, holly, laurel, peach, iris, and bead-beans. This he did as an education for his only daughter. Morning-glory started to grow of its own accord along the reed fence, but Fuji-ichi said that if it was a question of beauty such short-lived things were a loss, and in their place he planted runner-beans, whose flowers he thought an equally fine sight. Nothing delighted him more than watching over his daughter. When the young girl grew into womanhood he had a marriage screen constructed for her, and since he considered that one decorated with views of Kyoto would make her restless to visit the places she had not yet seen, and that illustrations of "The Tale of Genji" or "The Tales of Ise" might engender frivolous thoughts, he had the screen painted with busy scenes of the silver and copper mines at Tada. He composed Instructional Verses on the subject of economy and made his daughter recite them aloud. Instead of sending her to a girls' temple school, he taught her how to write himself, and by the time he had reached the end of his syllabus, he had made her the most finished and accomplished girl in Kyoto. Imitating her father in his thrifty ways, after the age of eight she spilt no more ink on her sleeves, played no longer with dolls at the Doll Festival, nor joined in the dancing at Bon.* Every day she combed her own hair and bound it in a simple bun. She never sought others' help in her private affairs. She mastered the art of stretching silk padding and learned to fit it perfectly to the length and breadth of each garment. Since young girls can do all this if properly disciplined, it is a mistake to leave them to do as they please.

Once, on the evening of the seventh day of the New

---

* A summer festival.

Year, some neighbors asked leave to send their sons to Fuji-ichi's house to seek advice on how to become millionaires. Lighting the lamp in the sitting room, Fuji-ichi set his daughter to wait, bidding her let him know when she heard a noise at the private door from the street. The young girl, doing as she was told with charming grace, first carefully lowered the wick in the lamp. Then, when she heard the voices of the visitors, she raised the wick again and retired to the scullery. By the time the three guests had seated themselves the grinding of an earthenware mortar could be heard from the kitchen, and the sound fell with pleasant promise on their ears. They speculated on what was in store for them.

"Pickled whaleskin soup?" hazarded the first.

"No. As this is our first visit of the year, it ought to be rice-cake gruel," said the second.

The third listened carefully for some time, and then confidently announced that it was noodle soup. Visitors always go through this amusing performance. Fuji-ichi then entered and talked to the three of them on the requisites for success.

"Why is it that today is called the Day of the Seven Herbs?" one asked him.

"That was the beginning of economy in the Age of the Gods: it was to teach us the ingredients of a cheap stew."

"Why do we leave a salted bream hanging before the God of the Kitchen Range until the sixth moon?" asked another.

"That is so that when you look at it at meal time you may get the feeling of having eaten fish without actually doing so."

Finally he was asked the reason for using thick chopsticks at the New Year.

"That is so that when they become soiled they can be scraped white again, and in this way one pair will last the whole year.

"As a general rule," concluded Fuji-ichi, "give the closest attention to even the smallest details. Well now, you have kindly talked with me from early evening, and it is high time that refreshments were served. But not to provide refreshments is one way of becoming a millionaire. The noise of the mortar which you heard when you first arrived was the pounding of starch for the covers of the Account Book."

Bushido: The Feudal Ethic

The Tokugawa system provided the leaders of Japan after 1868 with a sound base upon which to build a modern nation. The affluent and frugal merchant we just met was a part of this base. Another legacy of the Tokugawa era was an educated and self-sacrificing samurai elite and, beneath it, a commoner class conditioned to unquestioning obedience to higher authority. The samurai had been rigorously trained in an ethical system which placed loyalty to one's lord at the apex of the value system. Though the formalization of this ethic in the Tokugawa period borrowed heavily from neo-Confucianism, the Japanese pattern differed markedly from the Chinese by clearly assigning family loyalty a position far below that of loyalty to one's lord. These attitudes of samurai and commoners contributed significantly to the rapid modernization of Japan; for it proved relatively simple to transfer the focus of loyalty and respect from the feudal lord to the emperor and the nation. Thereafter every Japanese could be expected, for the sake of emperor and nation, to match the self-sacrificing attitude described in the selection below.

In 1905, Inazo Nitobe, an American-educated Japanese of samurai descent, attempted to explain the feudal ethic (adapted for modern use) in his famous book, *Bushido: The Soul of Japan*. The following excerpt from the chapter on loyalty presents the sort of material which the students of Japan encountered regularly in their textbooks between 1870 and 1945.

INAZO NITOBE,
Bushido, pp. 82, 84–87

Feudal morality shares other virtues in common with other systems of ethics, with other classes of people, but this virtue—homage and fealty to a superior—is its distinctive feature. I am aware that personal fidelity is a moral adhesion existing among all sorts and conditions of men,—a gang of pickpockets owe allegiance to a Fagin; but it is only in the code of chivalrous honour that loyalty assumes paramount importance. . . .

[It is quite right to state] that whereas in China Confucian ethics made obedience to parents the primary human duty, in Japan precedence was given to loyalty. At the risk of shocking some of my good readers, I will relate of one "who could endure to follow a fall'n lord" and who thus, as Shakespeare assures, "earned a place i' the story."

The story is of one of the greatest characters of our history, Michizané, who, falling a victim to jealousy and calumny, is exiled from the capital. Not content with this, his unrelenting enemies are now bent upon the extinction of his family. Strict search for his son—not yet grown—reveals the fact of his being secreted in a village school kept by one Genzo, a former vassal of Michizané. When orders are dispatched to the schoolmaster to deliver the head of the juvenile offender on a certain day, his first idea is to find a suitable substitute for it. He ponders over his school-list, scrutinises with careful eyes all the boys, as they stroll into the class-room, but none among the children born of the soil bears the least resemblance to his protégé. His despair, however, is but for a moment; for, behold, a new scholar is announced—a comely boy of the same age as his master's son, escorted by a mother of noble mien.

No less conscious of the resemblance between infant lord and infant retainer, were the mother and the boy himself. In the privacy of home both had laid themselves upon the altar; the one his life—the other her heart, yet without sign to the outer world. Unwitting of what had passed between them, it is the teacher from whom comes the suggestion.

Here, then, is the scapegoat!—The rest of the narrative may be briefly told.—On the day appointed, arrives the officer commissioned to identify and receive the head of the youth. Will he be deceived by the false head? The poor Genzo's hand is on the hilt of the sword, ready to strike a blow either at the man or at himself, should the examination defeat his scheme. The officer takes up the gruesome object before him, goes calmly over each feature, and in a deliberate, business-like tone, pronounces it genuine.—That evening in a lonely home awaits the mother we saw in the school. Does she know the fate of her child? It is not for his return that she watches with eagerness for the opening of the wicket. Her father-in-law has been for a long time a recipient of Michizané's bounties, but since his banishment, circumstances have forced her husband to follow the service of the enemy of his family's benefactor. He himself could not be untrue to his own cruel master; but his son could serve the cause of the grandsire's lord. As one acquainted with the exile's family, it was he who had been entrusted with the task of identifying the boy's head. Now the day's—yea, the life's—hard work is done, he returns home and as he crosses its threshold, he accosts his wife, saying: "Rejoice, my wife, our darling son has proved of service to his lord!"

"What an atrocious story!" I hear my readers exclaim. "Parents deliberately sacrificing their own innocent child to save the life of another man's!" But this child was a conscious and willing victim: it is a story of vicarious death—as significant as, and not more revolting than, the story of Abraham's intended sacrifice of Isaac. In both cases was obedience to the call of duty, utter submission to the command of a higher voice, whether given by a visible or an invisible angel, or heard by an outward or an inward ear;—but I abstain from preaching.

The individualism of the West, which recognises separate interests for father and son, husband and wife, necessarily brings into strong relief the duties owed by one to the other; but Bushido held that the interest of the family and of the members thereof is intact,—one and inseparable. . . .

PART V. JAPAN BECOMES A MODERN NATION
(Meiji Period, 1868–1912)

Feudalism's Contribution to Modernization

On July 8, 1853, Commodore Matthew C. Perry of the United States Navy led an imposing naval squadron into Tokyo Bay and forced on the most unwilling Tokugawa shogunate a limited "opening" of Japan. The Japanese had managed to fend off earlier Russian and British efforts to open relations; but it was by now painfully clear to the shogunal authorities that they simply did not have the military means to maintain their self-imposed policy of isolation in the face of Western steamships and artillery. Following the United States lead, one by one the Western powers extracted concessions from the hapless Tokugawa. These "unequal treaties" (as the Japanese called them) outraged most samurai, in particular the granting of "extra territoriality" which provided that the Japanese could not try and punish Westerners for violation of Japanese laws.

During its final fifteen years the shogunate found itself in a tightening vise of irresistible Western demands and an increasingly serious internal threat. Actually, Tokugawa fortunes had been on the decline for many decades prior to Perry's arrival. As the power of the merchants had increased, the peasants suffered terribly under the demands of the samurai for increased agricultural output so that samurai could pay their debts to the merchants. Peasant revolts, invariably crushed, were common after 1800. A major economic reform was inescapable; but the Tokugawa bureaucracy had not risen to the challenge.

By the 1860s the Tokugawa government was being openly criticized both for the failure of its domestic economic reforms and, more significantly, for its inability to enforce its own isolation policy against the West. Ultimately, a coalition of powerful feudal domains, merchants (notably the house of Mitsui—still a great economic power in Japan), and officials of the imperial court forced the Tokugawas to relinquish power to the emperor. The slogan "Revere the emperor, expel the barbarians" was heard throughout the land.

The collapse of the shogunate before these forces in 1868 unleashed the drive for modernization which was to carry Japan to the status of a major world power by the turn of the century. Why was Japan the only Asian nation so rapidly to meet the West on its own industrial-military terms? Why should the Japanese have determined upon the need for radical internal change, while the Chinese clung to their traditional patterns?

As we see in the following selection, many features of the Tokugawa feudal structure contributed to the rapid modernization of the nation.

FAIRBANK et al.,
East Asia, pp. 181–186 (excerpts)

Insularity had from early times made the Japanese very much aware of their cultural and technological borrowings from the continent, even though the sum of such borrowings was probably no greater and possibly considerably less than in other countries of comparable size. Having early sent missions overseas to borrow from T'ang China, the Japanese were aware that useful things could be learned from abroad, and so found it easy to accept the idea of learning from the West. The Chinese normally assumed the opposite, and therefore were slow to appreciate what might be learned from the "barbarian" Occident.

The geographical isolation of Japan, as well as its distinctive language and feudal society, had also made the Japanese acutely aware that despite their heavy cultural debt to China they were a separate ethnic and political entity. In short, they already had a strong sense of separate identity which amounted to a feeling of nationalism. They assumed a plurality of countries in the world and made no claim to universal rule. In the nineteenth century, while the Chinese found the multi-state international system of Europe wholly unacceptable, the Japanese could quickly understand and accept it, and begin to act accordingly. . . .

In Japanese feudal society, status depended overwhelmingly on birth, and yet the Confucian political and social doctrines which permeated Japanese thinking asserted the moral potential inherent in all men. The contrast between hierarchi feudalism and some of the egalitarian doctrines of Buddhism was even greater. Thus there was not the same unity of theory and practice as in China and hence perhaps less stability. Ambitious men, if denied high status, would seek distinction through achievement. The energies that such stirrings produced were all the more dynamic because they were channeled within and subordinated to the ends of the group. In sociological terms, the Japanese can be called goal-oriented, the Chinese status-oriented. This is one reason why, in the face of the Western menace in the nineteenth century, many Chinese tried to control the situation by playing traditional roles, while the Japanese generally reacted by seeking specific objectives. . . .

While Chinese intellectuals generally excluded the West from their thinking, their Japanese counterparts were often avid for Western learning. Fear of Christianity had contributed to isolation in the seventeenth century; but once this threat had passed, the Japanese again became extremely curious about the West. In 1720 the ban was lifted on books about the Occident, so long as they did not deal with Christianity. Chinese books acquired through the Chinese merchants in Nagasaki were one source of information. Dutch traders were another. In fact, the Dutch language proved so important a source of learning about the West that the whole of Occidental scientific knowledge came to be known as "Dutch learning" (*Rangaku*).

Not only were the Japanese leaders much better informed than the Chinese about Western science; as feudal military men they had a more realistic understanding of military technology than did the scholar-gentry leadership of China. The Japanese did not have to be humiliated in bitter defeat before they could recognize their own military inferiority. At least some of them could see clearly, from the displacement of Western ships, the size and range of Western guns, and the strength of Western forces in the wars in China, that Japan was no match for the intruders.

Another underlying reason for the speed of the Japanese reaction was the relative smallness and accessibility of the islands and the close contacts maintained among all parts of the country. Perry's ships sailed within sight of Edo, the capital of the feudal government, and most of the other large cities were equally vulnerable from the sea. Although the country was divided into many autonomous feudal domains, the control system required the various lords and a large number of their retainers to spend alternate years in Edo (the *sankin kōtai* system). This brought the leadership into much closer contact than was afforded in China by the dispatch of officials from the capital to the provinces, even though the political structure of China was more highly centralized. Within a few weeks of Perry's arrival the whole country knew of this momentous event. Within four or five years, vigorous responses were coming from many areas, not merely from a few harried officials in a large bureaucracy or from residents of some port city remote from the capital.

Japan's responsiveness to Western contact seems

actually to have been a variety of responses, only some of which proved successful and emerged as the new trend. Just because of this greater diversity, Japan was better able than China to find and pursue lines of action that proved meaningful and effective.

The feudal system itself made for this greater variety of response. The Tokugawa political structure, unlike that of China, was composed of units of various degrees of autonomy. . . .

The responses at the imperial court, the shogunal capital, and the many castle towns of the major daimyo ran the gamut from intransigent opposition to open-minded acceptance of foreign intercourse.

Even the class divisions contributed to this diversity of response. . . . Samurai and commoners were kept strictly apart both socially and in their functions in society. Men raised as peasants or townsmen had no chance of political and social eminence, and so developed somewhat different concepts of economic enterprise and service than did most samurai. Their responses to Western stimuli often differed from those of the ruling class.

The wide diffusion of education also made for a diversity of responses. The samurai class, constituting some five or six per cent of the population, was roughly five times the proportional size of the degree-holding gentry class in China. It was no narrow feudal aristocracy of the European type but a rather broad upper class of education and traditions of leadership. . . .

The potential leadership was not limited to the samurai class. A high percentage of the urban merchant class was well educated as were also the richer peasants, who often represented long traditions of local leadership. Japanese literacy rates in the first half of the nineteenth century probably compared favorably with those of Western countries. Though little political leadership could be expected from the non-samurai elements, which had been strictly denied it by the whole Tokugawa system, a few individuals of peasant background and even some groups of peasants did have the temerity to join in the political controversies that resulted from the Western challenge. More important, the high educational level and experience in economic leadership of the urban merchants and rich peasants prepared them to seize opportunities in a time of upheaval.

Behind the various responses to Western contact we can discern a pervasive concern for the fate of the nation. The Japanese were determined to preserve their independence, and the concept of national interest, though variously understood, was a basis on which some responses were sorted out as more meaningful or effective than others, and accordingly found greater support, and shaped national policy. Certain reactions to Western technological superiority and military might did not work, whereas other efforts were highly successful and catapulted their advocates to positions of power.

For example, attempts to fight off Western ships with antiquated weapons were doomed to failure, but adoption of Western techniques was likely to get results. And in the Westernizing process, those who were willing to accompany technology by substantial political and social changes were apt to be more successful than those who refused to tolerate such changes. The *shishi* ["extremists" among the Samurai] who killed a foreigner and brought down retribution on his lord was likely to disappear from history after his one glorious moment; but the daring young samurai who went abroad to study might return to rise quickly by his new knowledge. Some restless samurai, disillusioned by their inability to drive out the foreigners, switched to advocate the development of national strength through further foreign intercourse, and by this new approach developed into prominent leaders.

To survive, Japan had to modernize its defenses and economy and achieve a more efficient and centralized political organization. Persons who had an anti-shogunate background could afford to be radical and revolutionary, since they had less reason to cling to the *status quo.* Among samurai with anti-Tokugawa backgrounds, those from large and effectively united *han* could win strong political and military backing, while those from small and divided or insolvent *han* [feudal domains] could get little such support. An interesting anomaly was that the large anti-Tokugawa *han* of Southwest Japan, from which the new leadership largely came, were economically and socially backward compared with much of the area under the direct rule of the Tokugawa and their "hereditary" vassals, but for this very reason were more cohesive feudal units and therefore more able to act effectively. Thus the overthrow of the shogunate and the subsequent modernization of Japan presents the strange picture of men with a relatively old-fashioned background leading a revolutionary change, while those from more advanced parts of the country meekly followed their lead. The result was a certain conservative-radical ambivalence in the whole movement.

The Charter Oath

When a fourteen year-old boy was made emperor of Japan in 1867 and took up residence in the newly designated capital, Tokyo (formerly Edo), he could not have imagined the outlines of the sweeping transformation that would take place during his forty-five-year reign. Meiji (enlightened ruler), the name given to his reign and posthumously to the man as well, proved an apt choice.*

Though the new government was referred to as the "restoration" of imperial rule, the actual decision making was carried out by a remarkably small group made up almost entirely of the young samurai from

---

* The imperial line has never had a family name. Even the given name (Mutsuhito in this case) is never used after accession—the Japanese simply say "the emperor" or "the empress" until the posthumous name comes into use.

the western domains who had led the fight against the Tokugawa. Though acts of violence and natural deaths gradually reduced their numbers, this "Meiji oligarchy" dominated the government until after World War I.

The new leadership, united in its determination to modernize in order to maintain independence, implemented one daring program after another. Within three years the feudal structure was abolished and an effective central government established. Far from "expelling the barbarians," the Meiji leaders sent study missions abroad by the score and hired Western advisers to provide instruction in everything from industrial technique to elementary education.

The abolition of feudalism, the modernization of the nation, and the maintenance of authoritarian rule are all foreshadowed in the Charter Oath issued in the name of the young emperor in April 1868. The first article was intended to assure the daimyos and samurai that they would be consulted. It was not intended to suggest a parliamentary system of government, though advocates of such a system advanced this interpretation in later years.

Text from RYUSAKU TSUNODA et al., eds.,
Sources of Japanese Tradition, II, 137

By this oath we set up as our aim the establishment of the national weal on a broad basis and the framing of a constitution and laws.

1. Deliberative assemblies shall be widely established and all matters decided by public discussion.

2. All classes, high and low, shall unite in vigorously carrying out the administration of affairs of state.

3. The common people, no less than the civil and military officials, shall each be allowed to pursue his own calling so that there may be no discontent.

4. Evil customs of the past shall be broken off and everything based upon the just laws of Nature.

5. Knowledge shall be sought throughout the world so as to strengthen the foundations of imperial rule.

The End of the Feudal Structure

After 1868, talk of "expelling the barbarians" was replaced by a much more realistic slogan: "Rich country; strong army." The conviction that Japan's continued independence depended upon "catching up" with the West in industrial-military development helped to persuade the samurai and daimyos that the feudal structure would have to be abandoned. In exchange for giving up their feudal privileges the daimyos and samurai were given bonds issued by the new government.

For the haughty samurai, forced to give up the swords and other symbols of their station, the transition to the new order was often painful. Most moved successfully into commerce, government, or the officer corps of the new conscript-based army; some became simple farmers, and some talked bitterly of the need to overthrow the misguided government. This last stirring of the feudal order came to an end when a revolt of discontented samurai was crushed by the new conscript army in 1877.

The dismemberment of the feudal structure began when the daimyos of the powerful domains which had led in the overthrow of the Tokugawas turned over their lands to the emperor. This excerpt from the memorial to the emperor submitted by the four daimyos reveals both the effort to substantiate the "restoration" theory and the dominant aim of achieving "equality" with the Western powers.

Text from R. STORRY,
A History of Modern Japan, p. 105

There is no soil within the Empire that does not belong to the Emperor . . . and no inhabitant who is not a subject of the Emperor, though, in the Middle Ages, the Imperial power declined and the military classes rose, taking possession of the land and dividing it among themselves as the prize of their bow and spear. But now that the Imperial power is restored, how can we retain possession of land that belongs to the Emperor and govern people who are his subjects? We therefore reverently offer up all our feudal possessions . . . so that a uniform rule may prevail throughout the Empire. Thus the country will be able to rank equally with the other nations of the world.

Enthusiasm for Westernization

Interest in Western culture and technology picked up rapidly after Perry's mission and grew in the first twenty years of the Meiji period until it seemed to reach every level of society. Probably the most influential individual contributing to popular enthusiasm for Western ways was Yukichi Fukuzawa. Fukuzawa made the first of many trips to the West in 1860 as a member of a mission dispatched by the shogunate. He became convinced of the need for wholesale modernization of Japan and devoted himself thereafter to popularizing this cause. His books on the subject were read by millions of Japanese. He founded a successful newspaper and a school which was to become one of Japan's most famous private universities. Fukuzawa never accepted a post in the Meiji government, but his influence was enormous. The following selections from his autobiography illustrate Fukuzawa's keen interest in the ways of the West. In his final comment on the need for encouraging religion ("either Buddhism or Christianity"), Fukuzawa reveals the pragmatic outlook which marked the approach of the Meiji leaders to an even greater degree. In looking for models, whether for battleships or constitutions, the Japanese chose carefully, and shrewdly adapted what they picked to their exact needs. The initial paragraph also reveals the intense national pride which provided much of the impetus for Japan's rapid development.

Text, by YUKICHI FUKUZAWA,
from RYUSAKU TSUNODA et al., eds.,
Sources of Japanese Tradition,
II, 118–121, 129–130

I am willing to admit my pride in this accomplishment
for Japan. The facts are these: It was not until the sixth
year of Kaei (1853) that a steamship was seen for the
first time; it was only in the second year of Ansei (1855)
that we began to study navigation from the Dutch in
Nagasaki; by 1860, the science was sufficiently understood to enable us to sail a ship across the Pacific. This
means that about seven years after the first sight of a
steamship, after only about five years of practice, the
Japanese people made a trans-Pacific crossing without
help from foreign experts. I think we can without undue
pride boast before the world of this courage and skill.
As I have shown, the Japanese officers were to receive
no aid from Captain Brooke throughout the voyage. Even
in taking observations, our officers and the Americans
made them independently of each other. Sometimes they
compared their results, but we were never in the least
dependent on the Americans. . . .

As I consider all the other peoples of the Orient as
they exist today, I feel convinced that there is no other
nation which has the ability or the courage to navigate
a steamship across the Pacific after a period of five
years of experience in navigation and engineering. Not
only in the Orient would this feat stand as an act of unprecedented skill and daring. Even Peter the Great of
Russia, who went to Holland to study navigation, with
all his attainments in the science could not have equalled
this feat of the Japanese. Without doubt, the famous
Emperor of Russia was a man of exceptional genius, but
his people did not respond to his leadership in the
practice of science as did our Japanese in this great adventure. . . .

While we were in London, a certain member of the

Parliament sent us a copy of a bill which he said he had proposed in the House under the name of the party to which he belonged. The bill was a protest against the arrogant attitude of the British minister to Japan, Alcock, who had at times acted as if Japan were a country conquered by military force. One of the instances mentioned in the bill was that of Alcock's riding his horse into the sacred temple grounds of Shiba, an unpardonable insult to the Japanese.

On reading the copy of this bill, I felt as if "a load had been lifted from my chest." After all, the foreigners were not all "devils." I had felt that Japan was enduring some pointed affronts on the part of the foreign ministers who presumed on the ignorance of our government. But now that I had actually come to the minister's native land, I found that there were among them some truly impartial and warm-hearted human beings. So after this I grew even more determined in my doctrine of free intercourse with the rest of the world.

During this mission in Europe I tried to learn some of the most commonplace details of foreign culture. I did not care to study scientific or technical subjects while on the journey, because I could study them as well from books after I had returned home. But I felt that I had to learn the more common matters of daily life directly from the people, because the Europeans would not describe them in books as being too obvious. Yet to us those common matters were the most difficult to comprehend.

For instance, when I saw a hospital, I wanted to know how it was run—who paid the running expenses; when I visited a bank, I wished to learn how the money was deposited and paid out. By similar firsthand queries, I learned something of the postal system and the military conscription then in force in France but not in England. A perplexing institution was representative government. When I asked a gentleman what the "election law" was and what kind of an institution the Parliament really was, he simply replied with a smile, meaning I suppose that no intelligent person was expected to ask such a question. But these were the things most difficult of all for me to understand. In this connection, I learned that there were different political parties—the Liberal and the Conservative—who were always "fighting" against each other in the government.

For some time it was beyond my comprehension to understand what they were "fighting" for, and what was meant, anyway, by "fighting" in peace time. "This man and that man are 'enemies' in the House," they would tell me. But these "enemies" were to be seen at the same table, eating and drinking with each other. I felt as if I could not make much out of this. It took me a long time, with some tedious thinking, before I could gather a general notion of these separate mysterious facts. In some of the more complicated matters, I might achieve an understanding five or ten days after they were explained to me. But all in all, I learned much from this initial tour of Europe.

After all, the present is the result of the past. This glorious condition of our country cannot but be the fruit of the good inheritance from our ancestors. We are the fortunate ones who live today to enjoy this wonderful bequest. Yet I feel as though my second and greater ambition has been attained, for everything that I had hoped for and prayed for has been realized through the benevolence of Heaven and the virtues of those forebears. I have nothing to complain of on looking backward, nothing but full satisfaction and delight.

However, it seems that there is no end to man's capacity for desire. I can still point out some things I am yet hoping for. Not ideas in foreign diplomacy nor developments in our constitutional government—all these I leave to the statesmen. But I should like to put my further efforts towards elevating the moral standards of men and women of my land to make them truly worthy of a civilized nation. Then I should like to encourage a religion—either Buddhism or Christianity—to pacify the minds of a large number of our people. And thirdly, I wish to have a large foundation created for the study of both the physical and metaphysical sciences.

It is these three things that I wish to see accomplished during the remaining years of my life. Though a man may grow old, he should keep active as long as he has his health both of mind and body. And so I intend to do all that lies within my power as long as it is granted to me.

Overenthusiasm for Westernization

The enthusiasm for Westernization encouraged so effectively by Fukuzawa as well as by government policy reached its peak in the early 1880s. Many Japanese acted as though they wished to disassociate themselves completely from their past. Educated city dwellers flocked to newly established Christian churches in such numbers that many Western missionaries predicted a "Christian Japan" by 1900. The clothing, social relations, and affectations of the Westerners were aped, often with comic results. There were even suggestions that Japanese should intermarry with Caucasians in order to "improve" the Japanese race.

The following piece was written during the period to parody the extreme enthusiasm for Western ways. Eating beef had been forbidden by Buddhist law, but its consumption became one of the marks of "enlightenment" after 1868.

———————

Text, by ROBUN KANAGAKI,
from DONALD KEENE, ed.,
Modern Japanese Literature, pp. 31–33

A man about thirty-five, rather swarthy it is true, but of clear complexion, thanks apparently to the daily use of soap, which purges all impurities. His hair, not hav-

ing been cut for some hundred days, is long and flowing, and looks as if it is in the process of being let out altogether, in the foreign style. Naturally enough, he uses that scent called Eau de Cologne to give a sheen to his hair. He wears a padded silken kimono beneath which a calico undergarment is visible. By his side is his Western-style umbrella, covered in gingham. From time to time he removes from his sleeve with a painfully contrived gesture a cheap watch, and consults the time. As a matter of fact this is merely so much display to impress others, and the chain is only gold-plate. He turns to his neighbor, who is also eating beef, and speaks:

Excuse me, but beef is certainly a most delicious thing, isn't it? Once you get accustomed to its taste, you can never go back to deer or wild boar again. I wonder why we in Japan haven't eaten such a clean thing before? For over 1620—or is it 1630—years people in the West have been eating huge quantities of beef. Before then, I understand, beef and mutton were considered the king's exclusive property, and none ever entered the mouth of a commoner, unless he happened to be something on the order of a daimyo's chief retainer. We really should be grateful that even people like ourselves can now eat beef, thanks to the fact that Japan is steadily becoming a truly civilized country. Of course, there are some unenlightened boors who cling to their barbaric superstitions and say that eating meat defiles you so much that you can't pray any more before Buddha and the gods. Such nonsense shows they simply don't understand natural philosophy. Savages like that should be made to read Fukuzawa's article on eating beef. In the West they're free of superstitions. There it's the custom to do everything scientifically, and that's why they've invented amazing things like the steamship and the steam engine. Did you know that they engrave the plates for printing newspapers with telegraphic needles? And that they bring down wind from the sky

with balloons? Aren't they wonderful inventions! Of
course, there are good reasons behind these inventions.
If you look at a map of the world you'll see some
countries marked "tropical," which means that's where
the sun shines closest. The people in those countries
are all burnt black by the sun. The king of that part of
the world tried all kinds of schemes before he hit on
what is called a balloon. That's a big round bag they
fill with air high up in the sky. They bring the bag
down and open it, causing the cooling air inside the bag
to spread out all over the country. That's a great inven-
tion. On the other hand, in Russia, which is a cold country where the snow falls even in summer and the ice is
so thick that people can't move, they invented the
steam engine. You've got to admire them for it. I understand that they modeled the steam engine after the flam-
ing chariot of hell, but anyway, what they do is to load
a crowd of people on a wagon and light a fire in a
pipe underneath. They keep feeding the fire inside the
pipe with coal, so that the people riding on top can
travel a great distance completely oblivious to the cold.
Those people in the West can think up inventions
like that, one after the other. . . . You say you must be
going? Well, good-bye. Waitress! Another small bottle
of sake. And some pickled onions to go with it!

Political Factions and Liberalism

The rather wild enthusiasms described in the preceding passage tapered off in the 1890s as the nation gained self-confidence. Still, the progress of
Westernization created complex problems for the Meiji leaders. Western technology was clearly necessary
as was the adoption of a degree of Western culture
sufficient to encourage the Western nations to abandon the hated "unequal treaties" which had been
forced upon the helpless Tokugawa government. Yet
some elements of the turn to the West represented

a clear threat to the Meiji oligarchy. In no area was the threat more obvious than in the interest of many educated Japanese in Western representative forms of government. Reversing the Western pattern, political parties came into existence in Japan *before* the establishment of a parliament. The initial impetus for this development was actually not provided by enthusiasm for liberal ideas, but rather by frustration over the fact that the Meiji government was dominated by ex-samurai from the former domains of Satsuma and Choshu. Some members of the oligarchy from other domains resigned from the government when their views were consistently ignored, and turned to the idea of a parliamentary system as a way of breaking the domination of the Satsuma-Choshu clique. Thus it came to be that many of the cherished ideals of Western liberals found expression on the Japanese political scene in the 1870s. The following selections are from a "Memorial for the Establishment of a Representative Assembly" presented to the government in 1874. The intense nationalism of the petitioners is revealed in their argument that an assembly is needed because it would encourage the people to "be of one mind" and thus strengthen the nation.

Text from w. w. MCLAREN, ed.,
"Japanese Government Documents,"
pp. 427–433

When we humbly reflect upon the quarter in which the governing power lies, we find that it lies not with the Crown (the Imperial House) on the one hand, nor with the people on the other, but with the officials alone. We do not deny that the officials respect the Crown, and yet the Crown is gradually losing its prestige, nor do we deny that they protect the people, and yet the manifold decrees of the government appear in the morning and are changed in the evening, the administration is conducted in an arbitrary manner, rewards and punishments are prompted by partiality, the channel by which the people should communicate with the government is blocked up and they cannot state their grievances. Is it to be hoped that the empire can be perfectly ruled in this manner? An infant knows that it cannot be done. We fear, therefore, that if a reform is not effected the state will be ruined. Unable to resist the promptings of our patriotic feelings, we have sought to devise a means of rescuing it from this danger, and we find it to consist in developing public discussion in the empire. The means of developing public discussion is the establishment of a council-chamber chosen by the people. Then a limit will be placed to the power of the officials, and both governors and governed will obtain peace and prosperity. We ask leave then to make some remarks on this subject.

The people whose duty it is to pay taxes to the government possesses the right of sharing in their government's affairs and of approving or condemning. This being a principle universally acknowledged it is not necessary to waste words in discussing it. We therefore humbly pray that the officials will not resist this great truth. Those who just now oppose the establishment of a council-chamber chosen by the people say: "Our people are wanting in culture and intelligence, and have not yet advanced into the region of enlightenment. It is too early yet to establish a council-chamber elected by the people." If it really be as they say, then the way to give to the people culture and intelligence and to cause them to advance swiftly into the region of enlightenment is to establish a council-chamber chosen by the people.

For in order to give our people culture and intelligence and to cause them to advance into the region of enlightenment, they must in the first place be induced to protect their rights, to respect and value themselves, and be inspired by a spirit of sympathy with the griefs and joys of the empire, which can only be done by giving them a voice in its concerns. It has never happened that under such circumstances the people have been content to remain in a backward condition or have been satisfied with want of culture and intelligence. . . .

We believe that the intelligence of the officials must have made progress as compared with what it was previous to the Restoration, for the intelligence and knowledge of human beings increase in proportion as they are exercised. Therefore to establish a council-chamber chosen by the people would promote the culture and intelligence of the people and cause them to advance rapidly into the region of enlightenment. The duty of a government and the object which it ought to promote in the fulfillment of that duty is to enable the people to make progress. . . .

How is the government to be made strong? It is by the people of the empire becoming of one mind. . . .

Constitutional Development in the Emperor's Name

The Meiji leaders' response to the demands for an assembly revealed their shrewdness. They acceded to the demand for a parliament; but took the whole issue out of the public arena by having the sacrosanct emperor himself take on the duty of devising the new system. To raise questions after the issuing of the following rescript in 1881 was to risk open disrespect. Such use of the imperial throne by the Meiji leaders was frequently employed to silence criticism.

Text from w.w. MCLAREN, ed.,
"Japanese Government Documents,"
pp. 86–87.

We, sitting on the Throne which has been occupied by Our dynasty for over 2500 years, and now exercising in Our name and right all authority and power transmitted to us by Our ancestors, have long had in view gradually to establish a constitutional form of government, to the end that Our successors on the Throne may be provided with a rule for their guidance.

It was with this object in view that in the 8th year of Meiji we established the Senate, and in the 11th year of Meiji authorized the formation of Local Assemblies, thus laying the foundation for the gradual reforms which We contemplated. These Our acts must convince you, Our subjects, of Our determination in this respect from the beginning.

Systems of government differ in different countries, but sudden and unusual changes cannot be made without great inconvenience.

Our ancestors in Heaven watch Our acts, and We recognise Our responsibility to them for the faithful discharge of Our high duties, in accordance with the principles, and the perpetual increase of the glory, they have bequeathed to Us.

We therefore hereby declare that We shall, in the 23rd year of Meiji, establish a Parliament, in order to carry into full effect the determination We have announced, and We charge Our faithful subjects bearing Our commissions to make, in the mean time, all necessary preparations to that end.

With regard to the limitations upon the Imperial prerogative, and the constitution of the Parliament, We shall decide hereafter and make proclamation in due time.

We perceive that the tendency of Our people is to advance too rapidly, and without that thought and consideration which alone can make progress enduring, and We warn Our subjects, high and low, to be mindful of Our will, and that those who may advocate sudden and violent changes, thus disturbing the peace of Our realm, will fall under Our displeasure.

We expressly proclaim this to Our subjects.

The Meiji Constitution

The emperor's promise of a representative assembly was redeemed in 1890 when a constitution was bestowed upon the nation by the emperor himself. As the following excerpts reveal, the Meiji Constitution provided ample safeguards against a runaway progress toward democracy. The powers reserved to the emperor guaranteed the Meiji oligarchy continued control from their unassailable position behind the throne. For all its limitations, however, the Meiji Constitution did provide Japan with a parliamentary apparatus quite familiar to Western observers.

Text from ITO HIROBUMI,
Commentaries on the Constitution of the Empire of Japan

Preamble. Having, by virtue of the glories of Our Ancestors, ascended the Throne of a lineal succession unbroken for ages eternal; desiring to promote the welfare of, and to give development to the moral and intellectual faculties of Our beloved subjects, the very same that have been favored with the benevolent care and affectionate vigilance of Our Ancestors; and hoping to maintain the prosperity of the State, in concert with Our people and with their support, We hereby promulgate, in pursuance of Our Imperial Rescript of the 12th day of the 10th month of the 14th year of Meiji, a fundamental law of State, to exhibit the principles, by which We are to be guided in Our conduct, and to point out to what Our descendants and Our subjects and their descendants are forever to conform.

The rights of sovereignty of the State, We have inherited from Our Ancestors, and We shall bequeath them to Our descendants. Neither We nor they shall in future fail to wield them, in accordance with the provisions of the Constitution hereby granted.

We now declare to respect and protect the security of the rights and of the property of Our people, and to secure to them the complete enjoyment of the same, within the extent of the provisions of the present Constitution and of the law.

The Imperial Diet [legislature] shall first be convoked for the 23rd year of Meiji and the time of its opening shall be the date when the present Constitution comes into force.

When in the future it may become necessary to amend any of the provisions of the present Constitution, We or Our successors shall assume the initiative right, and submit a project for the same to the Imperial Diet. The Imperial Diet shall pass its vote upon it, according to the conditions imposed by the present Constitution, and in no otherwise shall Our descendants or Our subjects be permitted to attempt any alteration thereof.

Our Ministers of State, on Our behalf, shall be held responsible for the carrying out of the present Constitution, and Our present and future subjects shall forever assume the duty of allegiance to the present Constitution.

Chapter I. The Emperor. Article I. The Empire of Japan shall be reigned over and governed by a line of Emperors unbroken for ages eternal.

Article II. The Imperial Throne shall be succeeded to by Imperial male descendants, according to the provisions of the Imperial House Law.

Article III. The Emperor is sacred and inviolable.

Article IV. The Emperor is the head of the Empire, combining in Himself the rights of sovereignty, and exercises them, according to the provisions of the present Constitution.

Article V. The Emperor exercises the legislative power with the consent of the Imperial Diet.

Article VI. The Emperor gives sanction to laws and orders them to be promulgated and executed.

Article VII. The Emperor convokes the Imperial Diet,

opens, closes and prorogues it, and dissolves the House of Representatives.

Article VIII. The Emperor, in consequence of an urgent necessity to maintain public safety or to avert public calamities, issues, when the Imperial Diet is not sitting, Imperial Ordinances in the place of law.

Such Imperial Ordinances are to be laid before the Imperial Diet at its next session, and when the Diet does not approve the said Ordinances, the Government shall declare them to be invalid for the future.

Insurance Against Excessive Liberalism

The Meiji leaders fully realized the importance of education. Public schools were established as rapidly as funds and personnel permitted and by 1905, 95 percent of the children of primary school age were in schools.

From the outset the schools were used to inculcate values as well as to teach skills. This was especially so after the mid-1880's when the government, reacting to the enthusiasm for Western ideas, increasingly used the schools to indoctrinate the masses with the spirit of nationalism, loyalty to the emperor, and respect for authority. A major step in this program was the issuing of the imperial rescript on education in 1890. The rescript was read regularly in the schools and soon was familiar to every Japanese. There was such a sacred aura accompanying these readings and the associated bow to the imperial portraits that a white-gloved school official who stumbled in his presentation was likely to tender his resignation.

The rescript, permeated with Confucian ideals, stresses loyalty and acceptance of the status quo. Political agitation could hardly accord with the precepts presented here. Of even greater importance than the content of the document, however, is the implicit recognition by the government of the utility of public education as an instrument in the formation of national character.

Text from *The Japan Year Book 1939–1940*,
p. 633

Know ye, Our Subjects!

Our Imperial Ancestors have founded Our Empire on a basis broad and everlasting and have deeply and firmly implanted virtue; Our subjects, ever united in loyalty and filial piety, have from generation to generation illustrated the beauty thereof. This is the glory of the fundamental character of Our Empire, and herein also lies the source of Our education. Ye, Our subjects, be filial to your parents, affectionate to your brothers and sisters; as husbands and wives be harmonious, as friends true; bear yourselves in modesty and moderation; extend your benevolence to all; pursue learning and cultivate arts, and thereby develop your intellectual faculties and perfect your moral powers; furthermore, advance the public good and promote common interests; always respect the Constitution and observe the laws; should any emergency arise, offer yourselves courageously to the State; and thus guard and maintain the prosperity of Our Imperial Throne, coeval with heaven and earth. So shall ye not only be Our good and faithful subjects, but render illustrious the best traditions of your forefathers.

The way here set forth is indeed the teaching bequeathed by Our Imperial Ancestors, to be observed alike by Their Descendants and subjects, infallible for all ages and true in all places. It is Our wish to lay it to heart in all reverence, in common with you. Our subjects, that we may all thus attain to the same virtue.

The 30th day of the 10th month of the 23rd year Meiji.

Economic Development

The economic development of Meiji Japan and the growth of military power which it permitted were a source of wonder to contemporary observers. The possible relevance of the Japanese experience to the currently "developing" nations has engendered increasing interest in recent years.

From our present perspective it seems remarkable that Japan's modernization was financed largely from domestic sources. The rural population bore the major burden in the early decades. Not only were land taxes high, but most of the income so raised was devoted to the development of basic industry rather than improvement in social welfare. The now familiar pattern of rapid population growth in a developing nation ensured an ample labor force for industry and the maintaining of a competitive advantage in trade through relatively low wages.

The following selection discusses several key aspects of Japan's economic development and assesses their relevance to the developing nations today. Of particular interest are the role of government and the two-edged sword of nationalism.

W. W. LOCKWOOD, in H. PUSSIN, ed.,
The United States and Japan, pp. 96–100

First the time-scale should not be underestimated. Japan's success story is a story of 50–75 years, not of two or three spectacular five-year plans. At any point of time in her modern century—1880, 1910, 1925—contemporary observers saw no revolutionary gain over the previous decade nor any cause for optimism over the future. In the end, the Japanese tripled their production of goods and services per capita through the five decades 1885–1935. (National income rose by 3 per cent or more a year and its per capita level about 2 per cent—high rates by world standards for such a long period.) But this was only through the unremitting toil of a disciplined nation under determined leadership over three generations.

Other newly modernizing nations may do better today; India's progress since 1950, for example, is impressive by comparison, as is that of other countries like Thailand and the Philippines. They have new techniques for forcing economic growth and inputs of foreign aid such as Japan never enjoyed. On the other hand, they labor under certain offsetting handicaps. For one thing, their populations presently grow at 2.3 per cent a year rather than at Japan's prewar rate of a little above 1 per cent. Unless this rate can be checked there is likely to be a great pile-up of people in an already overcrowded agriculture. Japan just managed to avoid this fate by a more modest growth of population and by siphoning off her labor increment into rapidly expanding industries. Moreover, unlike Japan, today's newly developing nations are also embarking upon industrialization only after mass expectations have been aroused for a voice in politics for the redress of long-standing grievances and a share in the fruits of development. This complicates the joint tasks of growth, unity, and order in some respects, although it eases them in others.

At any rate, Japan's historic achievement seems impressive in retrospect. It shows that the industrial revolution of modern times, sustained over several decades, can lift a people far above traditional levels of poverty, ignorance, and disease, provided they give it a determined priority over other goals. Moreover, it shows that economic development under an efficient blend of public and private initiatives can have a cumulative, even accelerating character, as it matures. Today Japan's stepped-up growth is widening even further the gap between her and the rest of Asia. By the same token she is closing the lead of the more advanced industrial nations of the West.

The importance of continuity in development is further underscored by Japan's nineteenth century transition from traditional to modern institutions. Increasingly, historians attribute her success after 1868 to the assets she carried over into the modern era from her feudal past. . . .

Thus Japanese economic history offers little support to today's fashionable doctrine of "take-off," if this means that successful development is best achieved by some massive, revolutionary break-through—"development at one stroke." On the contrary, her growth in modern times links up with forces set in motion during the Tokugawa era. And it proceeds after 1868 in step-by-step sequences that begin slowly, and in varying degrees, to energize all sectors of the economy in interacting processes. No single industry or innovation is critical. No major sector of the economy jumps suddenly forward—except foreign trade. Nor are economic and social overheads like modern banks or public health facilities or joint-stock companies already present as "preconditions." They are created in the growth process itself. Much of the early gain in national income occurs actually in agriculture and other household trades, although of course it is facilitated in these traditional sectors by big structural innovations like the factory system, savings banks, universal primary education, and electric power.

The most striking discontinuity in Japan's modernization was political, not economic; for the Meiji Restoration of 1868 did make a decisive break with the past. In place of the confused and hesitant Tokugawa rulers, it brought to power a group of energetic young samurai determined to face the challenge of the West and committed increasingly to building a powerful, modern state on the foundations of an industrializing society. Yet even this political revolution had a gradual, unfolding character. Those who made it retained strong roots in the past and strong attachments to many of the values of old Japan.

In politics as in economics, then, one sees elements of continuity working persistently down to the present day to give strength and legitimacy to changes that are nevertheless silently coming on and remaking the country from one generation to the next. This capacity to effect orderly but massive alterations in society without rejecting entirely the past— indeed, making use of it—seems to be the genius of the Japanese. It was displayed most dramatically in the Meiji Restoration, and once again in Japan's post-1945 renaissance from defeat and devastation.

Current discussion of the interrelations of development and democracy in modernizing countries often cites Japan to show the virtues of authoritarianism, especially authoritarian nationalism, in the early stages of growth. There is some truth in this, of course, when it comes to the forced mobilization of savings for development and the rapid destruction of vested interests, traditional institutions, and attitudes that stand in the way.

To cite Japan in support of absolutism, however, is to tell only half the story. The political leaders of prewar Japan and their rising business allies led the country up the path of development, not merely because they wielded great power in the name of the Emperor but because they were progressive in their attitude toward technical development and instrumentalist in their views of how to achieve national and personal goals of wealth and power. Also, the society was open and fluid enough to permit a steady widening of opportunity in education, in economic life, and even to some extent in politics. This drew more and more people into the modernization process, gave it mass power increasingly, and slowly broadened its political foundations.

Many a ruling oligarchy elsewhere, no less despotic than the Japanese, has proved far less efficient in modernization because of various handicaps: a rigid traditionalism, blinders of revolutionary dogmatism, an exclusivist monopoly of power, or a fierce nationalism that stultifies rather than energizes development. These tendencies were not absent in prewar Japan. In considerable measure, however, they were held in check by convergence of forces pushing the country forward in the absorption of modern technology, and by counter-

vailing balances that developed within the ruling oligarchy to force the sharing of power among divergent elements—aristocrat and commoner, civilian and military
man, bureaucrat and politician, farmer and industrialist.

A major qualification of this statement must be made
with regard to the illiberalism and economic waste of
imperialism as it arose in military-rightist quarters and
finally took possession of the government in the Thirties.
Through the reign of the Meiji emperor (1867–1912)
nationalism served a constructive purpose on the whole.
It united the Japanese in building a nation state and
defending it against threats from abroad. The military
spending that it engendered may even have speeded
industrialization, since it remained limited in scale and
helped to introduce modern technology in arsenals,
shipyards, and machine industries.

After 1912, the social justifications of ardent nationalism are less apparent. As it passed from its defensive
phase to more aggressive chauvinism it was used to
rally popular support for the military against the rising
pressures of responsible civil government. At home it
remained the moral bulwark of resistance by conservative ruling groups to liberal, welfare democracy—at the
cost of economic efficiency no less than of social well-
being. Abroad it was employed to energize, step-by-step,
a process of empire-building. Here, increasingly, it wasted
a precious margin of resources, twisted economic growth
away from lines of comparative advantage, and left
government budgets perennially starved for other social
purposes. In the end, of course, it inspired the military
counter-revolution of the Thirties that took the nation
down the road to war. The Japanese now turned their
backs on liberal economic policies that had enriched
them for half a century and plunged into a vain effort
to build a self-sufficient empire in Asia.

Postwar Japan, like postwar Germany, is striking testi-
mony to the liberating impulse that can flow from lifting
a great military burden off the backs of people and

turning resources to productive investment and social welfare.

One other aspect of Japan's politico-economic tradition is of special interest today in view of experiments elsewhere in the developing world. This is her characteristic pattern of economic enterprise, joining substantial reliance on private initiative and the market mechanism with pervasive government influences that shape the broad lines of development. Perhaps the term "sponsored capitalism" best characterizes this Japanese mix of public and private responsibility. But it hardly suggests the shifting balance that developed historically between the two.

Initially, the Meiji state took an active hand in pioneering the new technology of modern, capitalistic industry. It shouldered risks and put up the capital for all sorts of ventures—mines, factories, shipping, railways, etc. Rather quickly, however, it drew back from most of its owner-manager responsibilities, leaving the main tasks of industrial enterprise from 1885 on to a rising business class coming forward in response to the new opportunity and the institutional facilities created by the regime. Thereafter it occupied itself mostly with strategic levers of influence, especially in banking and foreign trade, and above all to further military industries, colonial development, and other Imperial stakes. It was careful also to refrain from debauching the currency in reckless flights of inflation such as stultify progress in many developing nations today.

From rather timid beginnings, meanwhile, private business grew steadily in scale and capacity. This was true both of great industrial combines (*zaibatsu*) that developed in close partnership with the government, and of the myriad of small enterprisers who continued to dominate agriculture and a large share of manufacturing industry and the services. The public industrial sector, never large, now shrank to small proportions except in the military-colonial sphere. Only the war crisis of the Thirties overturned the system and imposed a sweeping straitjacket of government management upon the whole economy.

This prewar system of economic enterprise had its wastes and inefficiencies, its cyclical booms and busts. It perpetuated gross inequalities between rich and poor, landlord and tenant, and employer and worker, long beyond the point where the means were available (but not the political will) to redress the balance through public action. Yet it was immensely productive; it slowly widened freedom and economic opportunity for great masses of people; it preserved cultural values from the past rather than wiping them out in totalitarian fashion; and it slowly created interests and capacities to bring power under more responsible public control. It thus laid the foundations for the new affluence and political democracy of postwar Japan.

"The planners of India," said an Indian recently, "have more to learn from Japan than any other country." Equally this might be said of Americans seeking to understand and assist in the modernization of the non-Western world today.

PART VI. LIBERALISM AND REACTION
(1918–1945)

Experiments with Imperialism

In the final years before his death in 1912 the Meiji emperor could look with pride on the achievements of his subjects. Japan could legitimately claim a position of equality with the great powers of the West. No longer was it necessary to import ships and locomotives, for Japanese factories could now do the job. Universal compulsory education had raised the literacy rate well above 90 percent. "Rich country; strong army" was no longer a slogan, it was a reality.

There was yet another area in which the Japanese had successfully followed the lead of the West— empire building. As early as the 1870s a few hotheads within and outside the government had pressed for a military campaign in Korea. The samurai revolt referred to earlier was caused in part by the government's refusal to proceed more rapidly with overseas expansion. However, the cautious oligarchs were as determined as the impatient ex-samurai to see Korea brought within Japan's sphere of influence. The Chinese, who had dominated Korea from ancient times, resisted Japanese pressure with the result that Japan declared war on China in 1894. After humbling the Chinese in a brief war of eighteen months, the Japanese exacted from the losers a withdrawal from Korea, the fertile island of Taiwan, and a sizable indemnity.

After this success it was clear that the major challenge to Japan's influence in East Asia was Russia, whose eastward expansion had brought her to the shores of the Japan Sea. By 1900 Russian and Japanese commercial operations were colliding in northern Korea. Encouraged by their success in the Sino-Japanese War the Japanese again took the offensive in 1904. All the world was astounded when the Japanese, albeit with frightful loss of life, captured the theoretically impregnable fortress city of Port Arthur (Dairen) in Russian-held Manchuria and later shattered the entire Baltic Fleet just as it was nearing the end of a trouble-plagued six-month journey from St. Petersburg. After little more than a year of war both combatants were ready for negotiations—the Russians faced revolution at home, and the Japanese had reached the end of both financial and manpower resources. The extent to which nationalistic feeling in Japan had grown was fully revealed when riots broke out in Tokyo to protest the terms of the peace treaty. Actually, Japan's military adventures were again rewarded. Russia left Japan the master of Korea and Manchuria and ceded to Japan the southern half of the island of Sakhalin. After five years as a virtual colony of Japan, Korea was formally annexed in 1910. As if to add a final blessing to these developments the First World War provided the impetus for an economic boom sufficient to more than pay the debts incurred in the course of the Russo-Japanese War. Japan, technically one of the Allies, confined her activities in large part to filling orders for equipment and moving into trading opportunities left vacant by the Europeans.

So, it seemed, the goals of the Meiji oligarchs had been achieved. Japan possessed a modern industrial base, an educated and fiercely patriotic populace, and even a modest empire.

Democracy or Totalitarianism?

The second half of Japan's "modern century" was to witness first a swing toward liberal democratic patterns and then the rise of ultranationalism and the utter devastation of the country in 1945. It should not be assumed that the catastrophe brought on by Japanese militarism was somehow inherent in the plans of the Meiji leaders. The liberal trends of the 1920s testify to this fact. Yet the pendulum did swing in the 1930s toward totalitarianism and military aggression. What accounts for the shifts from the authoritarianism of the Meiji period to the liberal trends of the twenties, and finally to the totalitarianism of the thirties?

The author of the following selection sees the rise and fall of liberal democratic trends partly as the result of a long-term conflict between two forces produced by the process of modernization in any society. On the one hand he sees the "pull toward closer integration and greater authoritarian control of society," and on the other, "the pull toward individual liberties and democratic rights."

EDWIN O. REISCHAUER,
The United States and Japan,
pp. 190–198, 200–203 (excerpts)

By the 1920's the new forces unleashed by the Meiji reforms—one might better say the Meiji Revolution—were finally felt in their full power, and at the same time the growing divergence of the two paths down which they were leading Japan became apparent. Until the First World War the ultimate leadership had been in the hands of the old oligarchs, themselves products of the feudal age, who had started the revolution and had not been created by it. But with their disappearance from the stage, the Japanese Revolution came to full fruition, as leadership passed into the hands of men who were products of the revolution. The link with the past suddenly melted away. Japan was clearly out of sight of the stability of feudal times, and there was no way back. More important, the unity which the common samurai background of the Meiji leaders had given Japan suddenly vanished. The second generation of leaders had no such bond of common experience. They were the products of different backgrounds—of party politics, of *zaibatsu* business enterprises [great industrial combines], of the rigid civil bureaucracy, or the regimented ranks of the military.

In this sense, the disappearance of the Meiji oligarchy marked a crucial turning point in the Japanese Revolution . . . The Meiji oligarchs—one might even call them the "old revolutionaries"—dominated the scene for five decades, first as titular heads of the government and then in the less precise but more highly venerated role of *genro* or "elder statesmen." The *genro* system was typically Japanese—a product of the Japanese respect for age and dislike of the ostentatious display of power or of positions involving individual responsibility. Time after time in Japanese history, the real leaders have been a group of men behind the figurehead ruler or possibly behind a whole series of figureheads. It was altogether in keeping with the Japanese tradition for [the oligarchs] to withdraw behind the scenes as "elder statesmen" in order to avoid the petty annoyances and dangers of public life while still retaining ultimate control over the premiers and cabinets which held the limelight. But the oligarchs could not live forever. . . .

The First World War, coinciding as it did with the disappearance of the older leadership, gave tremendous impetus to the drive toward democracy and greater individual freedom. The victory of the three great democracies of the West—Great Britain, France, and the United States—and the collapse of the three more authoritarian states—the German, Austro-Hungarian, and Russian Empires—seemed positive proof that democracy was the vital force behind the amazing strength of the West. A wave of enthusiasm for democracy and internationalism swept Japan, bringing with it not only

Hara's* rise to the Premiership and the adoption of universal manhood suffrage but also Japanese withdrawal from Shantung and the Maritime Province of Siberia and the reduction in 1925 of the standing army by four divisions.

Perhaps more important than the First World War was the full-fledged development by this time of a significant new class which had been created by fifty years of Westernization. This was the urban white-collar class, or, as the Japanese more accurately call it, the *sarariman* ("salary man") class, produced by the need for technically competent and educated men in business, government, and the professions. Ranging from the university professor, doctor, and lawyer down to the shop clerk and office worker, this new urban class has dominated the culture of modern Japan even more completely than its cultural predecessor, the merchant class, dominated the arts and letters of Tokugawa times. Under its patronage the great city dailies, centered in Tokyo and Osaka, developed into powerful organs with circulations in the millions. Magazines of every degree of sophistication or vulgarity and every shade of opinion made their appearance together with a vast flood of books, as Japan became a nation of avid readers. Every artistic or philosophic current in the Western world produced its own little eddy in Japan. The urban intellectuals and white-collar workers found that education had opened for them the doors to the outside world, and they happily rushed out to bask in the light of a common world culture.

This was not merely a spiritual awakening. Growing intellectual independence inevitably produced in turn social individualism. Family authority began to disintegrate, as young people questioned the right of the family to choose their mates for them, thereby creating

---

* The first party politician to achieve the premiership without benefit of either samurai background or a Satsuma/Choshu heritage. (Ed.)

one of the most difficult of Japan's contemporary social problems. The younger generation joined in a world-wide social revolt, and Japanese flappers and their male companions, known respectively as *moga* and *mobo,* standing for the English words "modern girl" and "modern boy," delighted in shocking their elders. Some intellectuals began to question all authority, and a series of small radical movements sprang into existence. The spirit seeped down to members of the urban proletariat, another new class created by the Meiji reforms, and for a few years after the war Japanese industry was racked by strikes and labor disputes. Communism made its appearance among small groups of intellectuals, city workers, and even in some peasant communities. And in each successive election after the adoption of universal manhood suffrage, the white-collar residents of the cities showed their growing independence and disdain for established authority by voting in constantly growing numbers for socialist candidates.

A casual visitor to Japan in the 1920's might have concluded that the drift away from authoritarian traditions and toward political democracy and beyond that toward socialism would go on unchecked, as Japan followed the road blazed by the British in recent decades, but appearances were deceptive. Social individualism and political independence were largely confined to the cities, and democracy was infinitely feebler than in England. The Diet had won intermittent control over the cabinet, but its powers were still strictly limited. Even during the 1920's some cabinets were frankly nonparty governments, and, despite the limitation of naval expansion at the Washington Conference and the reduction of the standing army in 1925, there was doubt as to how fully the Diet and party cabinets could control the army, navy, or even parts of the civil bureaucracy. Still worse, the party system rested on a relatively narrow base and was sufficiently inefficient and corrupt to estrange the sympathies of many public-spirited Japanese. Electoral dishonesty was rampant, and Diet members were often venal servants of *zaibatsu* interests. And, in any case, the Diet for the most part represented only one narrow segment of the population, the small landowners and businessmen of the countryside, rather than the people as a whole. The backward peasantry and the equally impoverished city proletariat were unable to take full advantage of the vote, even when finally given it, and the city white-collar classes, while politically vocal, were inexperienced latecomers to the game of politics.

Thus, despite the obvious strength of the pull toward individual liberties and democratic rights, the conflicting pull toward closer integration and greater authoritarian control of society proved the stronger of the two forces which emerged from Westernization. However emancipated, intellectually and socially, the better educated residents of the cities might be, the mass of Japanese tenant farmers and day laborers unconsciously continued in the old paths of quiet obedience and deference to authority, and the vast weight of tradition still stood firmly in the way of democratic growth. Perhaps even more important was the mounting strength of the new forces of authority and conformity which Westernization itself had fostered—the highly centralized economic empires of the *zaibatsu*, the huge and omnipresent civil bureaucracy, the all-seeing, all-knowing police, and, worst of all, the closely knit and fanatical corps of army officers.

All of these enjoyed more or less independence of the forces of democracy as manifested in the Diet. The *zaibatsu* scarcely feared it, for they bought and sold Diet members themselves. And the fiction that the Emperor actually ruled and that the civil bureaucracy, army, and navy were his direct representatives gave the latter not only theoretical but often actual freedom from Diet control. The remaining *genro*, the Privy Council, and the whole high bureaucracy, which had succeeded the Meiji oligarchs as the men around the throne, stood both in theory and in practice above the elected representatives of the people. Through their figurehead, the Emperor, they had the power to choose premiers and to issue Imperial Ordinances. The Diet did not even have complete control over the purse strings, for the budget of the previous year continued in effect if the Diet refused to grant the government its new budget. Yamagata, the army builder and determined opponent of parliamentary government, had seen to it that the army and navy retained their independence. As early as 1895 a ruling was established that only active generals or lieutenant generals could serve as army ministers and similarly only active admirals or vice-admirals as navy ministers. This ruling, confirmed on two later occasions, gave the army and navy each a veto over any cabinet. By refusing to let one of their officers join it or remain in it, they could destroy any cabinet, whatever its backing in the Diet or bureaucracy.

The army perhaps best represented the totalitarian tendencies within the new Japan. Inheriting the warrior traditions of the samurai and all the prestige that a thousand years of feudal rule had given the soldier, it was a major link with Japan's authoritarian past, but more significantly it was an entirely modern product of Westernization and a chief shaper of modern Japanese totalitarianism. The new army of peasant recruits crushed the samurai revolts; it, more than any other major institution, broke down the old social classes and created a hierarchy of merit in which the sons of peasants could rise to the top; and finally it espoused many of the theories of socialism, championing the cause of the impoverished peasant against the wealthy urban industrialist. In short, the Japanese army, as seen against the background of Japanese feudalism, was almost as revolutionary an institution as the Diet itself. . . .

While this organization was in the hands of the samurai generals of Meiji times, it could be made a harmonious part of the total power structure of the state. But when its own propaganda-fed products began to reach the top, cooperation between the army and the Diet or even between the army and civil bureaucracy became difficult. The army officer simply lived in a different world from that of the party politician or civil servant.

Perhaps the most important area in which the two conflicting forces of democracy and totalitarianism met in Japan was in the field of education. Education was in a sense the key to Westernization itself. . . . But unfettered education not only taught men new skills but opened their eyes and made them think. . . . As the Japanese army discovered all too soon, indoctrination through modern educational facilities was an invaluable weapon for gaining power.

While education, thus, had helped produce the pull toward democracy in Japan, it was at the same time the strongest weapon in the arsenal of Japanese totalitarianism and the factor which above all others made any return to the feudal patterns of earlier times out of the question. Through the Ministry of Education the central government directly controlled the curriculums and teaching materials in every private as well as public school throughout the country. The key struggle between democracy and totalitarianism in modern Japan was the slow, hidden fight in the schools and newspaper offices. As education was gradually forced into the strait jacket of indoctrination, the triumph of totalitarianism became certain.

During the 1930's, the fight between the forces of democracy and totalitarianism came into the open in Japan, but only after the issue had already been settled. Despite the liberal, international flavor of city life during the 1920's, there had appeared unchallenged new dogmas of nationalism and new concepts of mystical authority, which were all the more powerful because of their vagueness. "Japanese spirit," "national polity" (*kokutai*), and other empty terms had been built up into solid realities in the public mind, and the violation of their undefined principles had been accepted as a heinous crime. Accusation of such a violation was enough to discredit the accused, for neither guilt nor innocence of such mystical crimes was susceptible of proof. People also had come to believe that there was such a thing as the "Imperial will," even though the Emperor carefully followed the dictates of his supposed advisors. A political fanatic or assassin could claim that he was following the "Imperial will" in opposing or even murdering the Emperor's ministers, and the public would condone his act.

Still worse, the inexperienced supporters of parliamentary rule in Japan saw no reason to defend the rights of minority groups. They saw no danger in the utilization of the powerful Home Ministry and the efficient, centralized police force it controlled to stifle freedom of speech, when beliefs they themselves did not share were involved. They even permitted the bureaucrats and police to establish the principle that it was a crime to think "dangerous thoughts." . . .

With the battle of intellectual freedom already lost, there was little hope that the forces of democracy would win, but even then the fight was long and confused. Other factors tended to overlie it and conceal the more essential struggle beneath. There was, for example, the dispute over foreign policy, which was in a sense merely one manifestation of the clash between these two forces. As we have seen, the world depression made the problem of Japanese foreign trade and empire more pressing, but the groups which favored foreign conquest were essentially the elements favoring totalitarianism within Japan, and the opposition was primarily the social groupings which stood behind democracy. The clash was precipitated by the dispute over the best methods of maintaining Japan's foreign trade, but behind it lay the more fundamental dispute over the basic organization of Japanese government and society.

The army's independence of the civil government permitted it to embark upon the seizure of Manchuria in 1931 and the conquest of all China in 1937, without the prior approval of government authorities or the people. . . .

> For Americans who tend to associate capitalism with a democratic system, the division of forces in Japan along economic and political lines presents a confusing and apparently inconsistent picture.

The Japanese army, drawing its strength from the less privileged rural classes, understandably became the champion of the peasants and the poorer classes in general. The army ideal was the traditional Japanese ideal of service rather than profit. Rich industrialists seemed to be wicked men to the Spartan army officers and their peasant recruits. The corruption of the Diet made possible an easy identification of avaricious capitalists with degenerate politicians, to the detriment of both. While the urban white-collar worker himself was drifting toward socialistic ideals, the rural radical distrusted the "city-slicker" socialist and tended to throw in his lot with the army. At the same time, capitalistic *zaibatsu* interests, while distrustful of army fanaticism and apprehensive about the military's program of foreign conquests, were more interested in suppressing popular radicalism and the labor movement than in forestalling the army's rise to power. Thus, the socialist-capitalist cleavage, though an important one in modern Japan, was not the principal rift in Japanese society. In the great struggle of the 1930's, socialists and capitalists stood firmly on both sides of the fence or attempted hopefully to straddle it. The real struggle was between democratic and authoritarian forms of government, as the bewildered and disorganized politicians of the older, conservative parties together with urban socialists bowed

before anti-capitalistic army officers, supported grudg-
ingly by pro-capitalistic bureaucrats and the great *zaibatsu* interests themselves.

It is disheartening to note how small a shift in the
balance of forces within modern Japan produced the
tremendous swing from the democratic tendencies of
the early 1920's to the totalitarianism of the so-called
Showa Restoration in the 1930's. The army, without
changing its basic views but merely by increasing its
intransigence, started the whole kaleidoscopic regroup-
ing of forces to form an entirely new pattern. Secure in
its virtual independence of the civil government and
emboldened by the growing economic crisis in the world
and the success of totalitarian ideas in Europe, the army
began to knock the props from under democratic government by "direct action." "Direct action" abroad meant
undeclared wars, which stirred up chauvinistic support
for the army within Japan. "Direct action" at home
meant political assassinations conveniently committed
by a lunatic fringe of officers and civilians but benefit-
ing the whole army's cause by intimidating the potential
opposition, party leaders, high bureaucrats, and *zaibatsu*
executives alike. The army had the tacit support of the
public, excited by the wars and as much blinded as
enlightened by the half-propagandistic education, it had
received, and public opinion was hard to resist in Japan,
where right and wrong were admittedly determined by
the judgment of society.

The other power groups in modern Japanese society
either adjusted to the army's strengthened stand or
meekly gave way before it. . . . Only the urban, white-
collar classes remained for the most part firm though
timidly silent advocates of democracy, voting heavily
for the few liberal candidates who were still allowed
to run in the now meaningless elections, but even in
this group there were serious defections, as many intellectuals climbed aboard the army's militaristic band
wagon and the urban socialist parties took on a strongly

totalitarian hue. And the masses of the people—the peasants and city workers—simply stood apathetically by, ready to follow whatever leaders should emerge. . . .

The struggle between democracy and totalitarianism was not merely a passing phase of prewar Japanese history. The fires of war and the surgery of defeat have brought physical and spiritual changes within the body politic of Japan, but this fundamental struggle goes on. The American occupation itself, with its educational programs and external controls, inevitably pulled in both directions. And when the occupation ended, the struggle went on, and it will unquestionably continue to go on for some years to come, determining in large measure the future of Japan and the role she will play in the world.

A Capitalist's Approach to Foreign Affairs

The attitude of Japanese big business toward foreign relations during the 1920s is illustrated in this selection from a speech made in December 1929 by an important executive in the giant Mitsubishi combine. It was views of this sort which caused ultranationalist fanatics to revile the capitalists and even to assassinate several major business leaders. A decade later, however, zaibatsu suspicion of the militarists had weakened as a result of the new business opportunities offered by the Manchurian conquests.

Text, by SOBUN YAMAMURO,
Ryusaku Tsunoda et al., eds.,
Sources of Japanese Tradition, II, 251.

When we consider [the state] of Japan's national economy, when we think of our scarcity of natural resources, when we reflect upon today's international situation, [the solution to our problems might seem to lie in] either the seizure of dependencies under a policy of aggression or the establishment of a Monroe Doctrine. Nevertheless, there is absolutely no place in Japan's future for [these policies]. Japan can keep itself a going concern only by means of international cooperation. Under this policy of international cooperation we can get along by producing goods of the highest possible quality at the lowest possible price, thereby expanding our foreign markets to the greatest [extent] possible. A country as deficient in natural resources as Japan buys raw materials from foreign countries at low prices and processes [these materials] at a low cost. Of course, circumstances peculiar to Japan have [modified] our development. For example, silk has been an important item. However, in addition to encouraging the expansion of this industry we must endeavor through a policy of international cooperation to establish our country as an international industrial producer of international commodities. To that end we must do our best to create an amicable atmosphere in international relations. If we have the reputation of liking war or of being militarists, [a policy of] international cooperation will be impossible. We must resolutely follow a policy of peace. It is essential to make all foreigners feel that the Japanese have been converted from their old religion and have become advocates of peace. For that reason we must as far as possible eliminate international barriers. In that sense, a commercial treaty with China is probably necessary. For this same purpose, the abolition of unnecessary tariffs is also required. I wonder if the best way to manage the post-resumption* financial world is not to eliminate the various international barriers, to adopt a viewpoint as similar as possible to that of the foreigner and to maintain close cooperation with foreigners.

---

* That is, after Japan returned to the Gold Standard, Jan. 1930.

Education and Indoctrination

The all-important role of education in molding public opinion has been noted in an earlier selection. In 1937, after the swing toward totalitarianism was well under way, the Ministry of Education issued a publication designed to provide ideological support for the government's program of military expansion and totalitarian controls. This excerpt from the *Fundamentals of Our National Polity* reveals the appeal to the legendary past for support of a view of the individual's relation to the state which would fit in any totalitarian society.

Text from RYUSAKU TSUNODA et al., eds.,
Sources of Japanese Tradition,
II, 280–281

Our country is established with the emperor, who is a descendant of Amaterasu Omikami, as her center, and our ancestors as well as we ourselves constantly have beheld in the emperor the fountainhead of her life and activities. For this reason, to serve the emperor and to receive the emperor's great august Will as one's own is the rationale of making our historical "life" live in the present; and on this is based the morality of the people.

Loyalty means to reverence the emperor as [our] pivot and to follow him implicitly. By implicit obedience is meant casting ourselves aside and serving the emperor intently. To walk this Way of loyalty is the sole Way in which we subjects may "live," and the fountainhead of all energy. Hence, offering our lives for the sake of the emperor does not mean so-called self-sacrifice, but the casting aside of our little selves to live under his august grace and the enhancing of the genuine life of the people of a State. The relationship between the emperor and the subjects is not an artificial relationship [which means] bowing down to authority, nor a relationship such as [exists] between master and servant as is seen in feudal morals. . . . The ideology which interprets the relationship between the emperor and his subjects as being a reciprocal relationship such as merely [involves] obedience to authority or rights and duties, rests on individualistic ideologies, and a rationalistic way of thinking that looks on everything as being in equal personal relationships. An individual is an existence belonging to a State and her history which forms the basis of his origin, and is fundamentally one body with it. . . .

War in the Pacific

Even during the 1920s many Japanese, especially in the military, questioned the wisdom of reliance on peaceful international trade to supply the needs of the Japanese nation. The Great Depression of the 1930s further convinced Japan's ultranationalists that safety for the country could only be assured by controlling sources of vitally needed raw materials.

To many of these men it seemed that Japan should move rapidly. China, more unified under Chiang Kai-shek than it had been in decades, was challenging Japanese economic interests in Manchuria, an area rich in iron and coal deposits. The Soviet Union was likewise building up its forces along the border of Manchuria.

In this setting, Japanese officers in Manchuria launched a military campaign against the Chinese without securing the approval of the civilian government in Tokyo. This inability of the civilian government to prevent "direct action" by the military paved the way to military domination of the government itself.

Censured by the League of Nations for their actions in Manchuria, where they had set up a puppet government, the Japanese simply withdrew from the hapless organization. Once again, as in 1895 and 1905, it seemed that military action had added to the wealth and security of the nation.

However, Japan's action had added fuel to the growing nationalism in China. In July 1937 Chinese and Japanese soldiers clashed near Peking. Again Japanese troops moved rapidly and within a year had captured every sizable city in China with the exception of the interior city of Chungking where the Nationalist government of Chiang Kai-shek remained until Japan's defeat in 1945.

The outbreak of war in Europe in 1939 left the United States as the only power in a position to prevent Japanese domination of Asia. In the early stages U.S. involvement took the form of aid to the Nationalist government of China. As the situation in Europe worsened the United States applied more direct pressure on Japan, first banning the sale of scrap iron to Japan and finally, with the aid of Britain and the Netherlands, shutting off oil shipments to Japan. The latter step placed Japan in a desperate position, for her military and industrial establishments would use up all oil reserves within a year. Japan had three alternatives: (1) to persuade the Allies to resume sales of strategic materials to Japan, (2) to secure the necessary oil by capturing the East Indies, (3) to take no action and die a slow death as the oil reserves diminished. The United States' position on the resumption of oil shipments was clear and inflexible— no oil unless the Japanese withdrew from China. To the militarists who had led Japan into China four years before, it was absolutely unthinkable to retreat before American pressure. Slow death from the lack of oil was no more acceptable. After a final round of negotiations with the United States in late 1941, the Japanese proceeded with the only remaining alternative—an expansion of the war. They attacked the U.S. Pacific Fleet at Pearl Harbor on December 7, 1941. None of the men who made the final decision to attack the United States were optimistic about the outcome. They simply regarded this course of action as less unacceptable than the other alternatives.

The Japanese at no time entertained the idea of invading the United States. Their hope was that they could rapidly consolidate their "Greater East Asia Coprosperity Sphere" stretching from Burma and Sumatra to Manchuria and then negotiate peace with a United States unwilling to pay the price necessary to dislodge them. Meanwhile, Hitler and Mussolini would see to it that no European power could threaten Japan's expanded empire. The Japanese achieved the rapid conquest envisaged by their plan. However, the two remaining assumptions in their program proved to be serious miscalculations: Hitler and Mussolini did not triumph in Europe, and the United States proved more than willing to pay the price of a major war in the Pacific. The price was high—especially for the Japanese.

Island by island the United States forces fought their way toward the Japanese homeland. Submarine and air attacks permitted little of the oil for which Japan had risked so much to reach the homeland. British forces turned back the Japanese in Burma. Between November 1944 and August 1945 almost every city in Japan was utterly devastated by fire-bombing B-29s. Finally, the dropping of two atomic bombs and the Soviet Union's entry into the war led the Japanese to surrender. A decisive role in this unprecedented decision was played by the man in whose name so many lives had been given—the emperor of Japan.

"Asia for the Asians"

The Japanese militarists represented their program of aggression, both to their own people and to the rest of Asia, as an idealistic campaign to remove the yoke of Western imperialism. The peoples of Asia were to enter a new era of prosperity under the benevolent direction of Japan. In point of fact, Japanese troops were welcomed by many colonial people, though enthusiasm soon changed to bitter hatred. Ironically, Japan, though destroyed in the process, did contribute directly to the end of Western colonialism in Asia. The propaganda line "Asia for the Asians," had appeal for many Indians, some of whom served under the Japanese against the British.

The following selection by a noted writer who supported the militarists reveals the ideological climate of the war years.

Text, by IICHIRŌ TOKUTOMI,
from RYUSAKU YUSAKU TSUNODA et al., eds.,
Sources of Japanese Tradition, II, 293–294

Now that we have risen up in arms, we must accomplish our aim to the last. Herein lies the core of our theory. In Nippon resides a destiny to become the Light of Greater East Asia and to become ultimately the Light of the World. However, in order to become the Light of Greater East Asia, we must have three qualifications. The first is, as mentioned previously, strength. In other words, we must expel Anglo-Saxon influence from East Asia with our strength.

To speak the truth, the various races of East Asia look upon the British and Americans as superior to the Nippon race. They look upon Britain and the United States as more powerful nations than Nippon. Therefore, we must show our real strength before all our fellow-races of East Asia. We must show them an object lesson. It is not a lesson in words. It should be a lesson in facts.

In other words, before we can expel the Anglo-Saxons and make them remove all their traces from East Asia, we must annihilate them. In this way only will the various fellow races of Greater East Asia look upon us as their leader. I believe that the lesson which we must first show to our fellow-races in Greater East Asia is this lesson of cold reality.

The second qualification is benevolence. Nippon must develop the various resources of East Asia and distribute them fairly to all the races within the East Asia Co-Prosperity Sphere to make them share in the benefits.

In other words, Nippon should not monopolize the benefits, but should distribute them for the mutual prosperity of Greater East Asia.

We must show to the races of East Asia that the order, tranquillity, peace, happiness, and contentment of East Asia can be gained only by eradicating the evil precedent of the encroachment and extortion of the Anglo-Saxons in East Asia, by effecting the real aim of the co-prosperity of East Asia, and by making Nippon the leader of East Asia.

The third qualification is virtue. East Asia embraces various races. Its religions are different. Moreover, there has practically been no occasion when these have mutually united to work for a combined aim. It was the favorite policy of the Anglo-Saxons to make the various races of East Asia compete and fight each other and make them mutually small and powerless. We must, therefore, console them, bring friendship among them, and make them all live in peace with a boundlessly embracing virtue.

Conditions on the Home Front

The following selections from a book written after the war by a Japanese Christian educator provide insights into wartime conditions in Japan. The first illustrates the effort of the government to build nationalism and emperor-loyalty during the 1930s. The date of the episode here described was April 21, 1937.

T. AIKAWA,
Unwilling Patriot,
pp. 3–7, 47–48, 81–88

On that unforgettable day when we had to welcome the Imperial Portraits—*Goshinei*—to our school, I stood on the hill where the school was situated and looked

down at the city of Yokohama. It was raining a little
and tiny raindrops were descending on the city like
small dust, the dust of sorrow and dismay. . . .

Until that day, Christian schools in Yokohama had
declined the proposal of the government that it provide
them with the Imperial Portraits; but the pressure became so great that they had to choose between closing
the schools or the acceptance of the proposal. To enshrine the Imperial Portraits in a school building was a
very common thing in Japan, a custom as old as the history of the schools themselves, but it suddenly became
a sort of supreme imperative for the schools after the
state of belligerency with China in 1932. Like the feudal
lords in the Tokugawa era who tested the religious belief of the people by making them tread on a copper
tablet of the crucifix, the Japanese government of those
days had begun to test the loyalty of school authorities
to the emperor and the state. . . .

At this time only a few schools were still showing
some resistance to accepting the Imperial Portraits, and
the government made up its mind in 1937 to crash the
last remaining ramparts with all its might and at one
blow. It succeeded everywhere; and the portraits were
also accepted.

In the afternoon of the day we accepted them, all
the pupils and students of our school, beginning with
the small boys of the high school department and up
to the big ones in college, lined up along the drive from
the school gate to the entrance of the main building. A
tense atmosphere reigned as each group of the boys
waited with great anticipation the coming of the car
of the president who was to bring the Imperial Portraits
from the prefectural office. In the silence of that hushed
mass, I heard raindrops fall from leaf to leaf in the
cherry trees planted along the path. Someone coughed
a time or two in order to escape from the unnatural
silence.

Time seemed to pass very slowly and sometimes almost stopped before the engine of the car was heard. Then the car stopped near the gate of the school. It was just one o'clock in the afternoon at the twenty-first of April, 1937.

An ex-officer teacher cried at the top of his voice: "*Saikei-rei!*" (Profound bow!)

Over the deeply bowed heads of the lines of boys, I saw the door of the car open and a white box appeared, held by the white gloved hands of the president of the school. The procession moved slowly between the lines of bowed heads and disappeared into the hall, leaving the faint sound of their shoes behind. I shivered a little, but I did not know why.

A kind of vigil for the Imperial Portraits began that night, and I had to take first duty because my name began with A—which means going first, even in Japan. *Hoanjo*, the sacred room for the Imperial Portraits, was built in the tower under the elaborate watchcare of the president. The Portraits were installed in a shrine-like box of plain wood with purple curtains on the outside. The Golden Chrysanthemum crest of the Imperial Family was shining above those purple curtains. Huge locks were placed on the box and on the door of the room itself. The place was, of course, "off limits" to all personnel except those on duty.

Four times during the night I had to go see that all was well, that nothing had been changed. I went from the first floor to the fifth with a light in my hand, walking through long corridors which gave no sign of any living thing, but reverberated with uncanny sounds. I dared not neglect my patrol since I had often heard that principals of public schools had committed suicide because of some damage done to the Imperial Portraits. Even natural disasters were not considered an excuse. I was honestly scared for I had no intention of committing suicide for the sake of a mere picture of a person to whom I had no personal attachment.

The Imperial Portraits were not the only things which

were a fatal threat to the life or position of a teacher. There was also the Imperial Rescript (*Kyoiku Chokugo*). Every school had a print of the Imperial Rescript, lent by the government. The most important duty of a principal was to read it on any and every public occasion. To make even a slight mistake in reading meant instant firing of the person responsible.

The organization of national effort reached down to the level of each Japanese through such groups as the one described below.

To choke off the least complaint and resistance, the government had invented and practiced a remarkable system of spying and enforcement. The system was called *Tonarigumi* (neighborhood group). It had its origin in *Goningumi* (five-man group) of the old feudal period under the Tokugawa Shogunate. The point of this *Goningumi* system was that everyone in the group was responsible for any crimes committed by any other members. If one committed murder, all five were under sentence of death. Thus the Tokugawa government prevented any uprising against the ruling class by the poverty-stricken people, especially the peasants. The wartime neighborhood group was the same as the older system. For instance, we were threatened with severe punishment if we failed to report to the town office any anti-war sentiment or comment in the neighborhood. The head of the group, consequently, had to know every detail of the private life of each member. When a woman was carrying a baby, she had to report this at once, and the head of the group determined her food ration.

In the second year of the war, instructions came from unknown sources to force us to have a small *Kamidana* or Shinto Shrine in our homes. The heads of most *Tonarigumi* inspected one home after another to check on any disobedient home that might have resisted the enshrining of the sacred symbol. The government office required a minute report of the weekly group meetings. These meetings continued until the air raids destroyed our city completely.

> The devastation wrought by the fire bombing of densely populated cities was stupefying, especially in the residential districts where wooden buildings predominated. Despite evacuation efforts undertaken as the raids grew in severity a total of 668,000 civilians were killed and 2.3 million homes were destroyed. Many small cities were as much as 95 percent destroyed in a single raid. Fires ignited by one raid over Tokyo killed 100,000 in a single night.
>
> Mr. Aikawa describes the climactic raid on the great port city of Yokohama.

A single B-29 flew over Yokohama about noon very high in the clear sky, from west to east. Its silver wings glittered beautifully in the May noonday sunshine. The toy-like smallness of that isolated glittering plane remained in my mind with strange vividness for a long time. But that day we did not know that this would mean the end of the old days, not only for our school, but for Yokohama itself.

A small group of students and teachers, who had been taking rest from factory work* on that twenty-eighth of May, 1945, worked very hard and with good spirit to put the final touches on a big pool to be used during a possible air raid on our school building. The weather changed during the night—a strange night without any air raid. I slept soundly and woke refreshed and strengthened the next morning.

An air raid siren went off in my school office about ten, but we were not too surprised for we had become accustomed to a morning air raid and called it "the morning mail." Almost every morning, after hearing the

---

* All school students in the country were engaged in war work on an almost full-time basis. [Ed.]

siren, we waited for the radio to tell us what damage had been done, whether great or small.

On that morning of the twenty-ninth, I could hear the roaring of engines in the distance but could not see the planes at all, because of the low hanging clouds, so different from the endless sky of deep blue of yesterday.

The radio began to speak: "Five hundred B-29s and one hundred fighting planes headed toward the Yokohama area; five hundred B-29s and . . ."

"Well, that is the biggest air raid we have ever had," I said as I took up my helmet and went out to see the enemy planes. At their desks, I noticed the colorless faces of the office girls whose eyes were saying, "Now this a real air raid. What shall I do? Where shall I go?"

I doubted my own eyes when I stepped out onto the roof garden. Board fences were already burning just where the streetcar line passed.

"Why the fire?" I cried. "Is that a part of the air raids?"

No enemy plane was to be seen, although the tearing sound of their engines was filling the air. Then I saw fire after fire started here and there, as though touched off by a magic invisible to our eyes. A very strong wave of rolling sound passed over our heads and then, with a sound like the scratching of a bamboo broom on sheet zinc, a countless number of fire bombs bounded like gigantic hailstones against the concrete building of our school and the stone-paved sidewalks alongside the classrooms. . . .

Fortunately an air-raid shelter was available.

When I first stepped out of the shelter, my eyes glimpsed multitudes of ragged people, walking with tottering steps toward the school building. Some were covered with blood, others with scorching quilts. They did not even know that the quilts with which they protected their heads were on fire. I shouted to them at the top of my voice to throw away the burning quilts lest they cause another fire in the building, and, when they did not hear me, I took the quilts by force and threw them away.

Most of them were muttering, *Namuami Dabutsu,* a kind of Buddhist invocation, believing that the prayer would help them. Even the children holding their parents' hands imitated their elders' prayers and walked on. They carried almost nothing with them, so sudden was the raid and so destructive the bombing. They were almost naked, too, for clothes were dreadfully quick to catch fire. So, with undiscernibly sooty faces, the dumb line of sad pilgrims passed by. They did not know where other members of their family were, nor even if they were alive or not.

Amidst the deadly moving shadows of those panic-stricken people, I saw a living tree suddenly catch fire just in front of our main building. Looking at the living leaves beginning to burn, I could not but believe that my end also might be near. My uniform would soon begin to dry to the ignition point, though several times I poured a bucket of water over myself. . . .

When evening came, I left the school, or rather the ruin of the school, to return to my house. The rumor was going around that no house had escaped the fire this time. Yokohama was no more on the face of the earth—only a vast field existed where the city of Yokohama had been. I went out by the back gate of our school, now only two base stones and a few charcoal blocks. I stumbled over something like burnt wood in the dusk. Looking down, I saw the charred remains of a man. This was the first, but soon I found the road almost completely covered with such human charcoal. I had to step over one after another to make my way out.

A mother lay headless with a baby on her back, holding one small girl by the hand. An old woman was breathlessly sitting on the pavement, her child on her lap. They seemed to be moving to and fro but, when I approached, they were dead—dead as Caesar.

Most shocking were those small charcoal bodies of children. They covered the ground like so many dead ants or flies. What were they thinking about just before their death? They surely called to their mothers. They surely waited for their mothers to come. And the mothers would never help them again.

Atomic Attack

When an atomic bomb exploded over the center of Hiroshima at 8:15 on a clear, hot August morning in 1945, approximately 64,000* people were instantaneously killed and some 72,000 injured, out of a total population of 255,000. Thousands more died from radiation sickness. Some seven thousand buildings were instantly leveled within a radius of approximately one mile from the blast center. Raging fires destroyed many buildings beyond the immediately affected area. Of forty-five hospitals in the city three were left standing. Only 28 of the 290 doctors in the city were unhurt.

Of the many accounts of the destruction of Hiroshima one of the most graphic is provided by the diary of one of the injured doctors who struggled to aid the horribly burned victims who flooded his half-destroyed hospital. His account of the efforts to understand and treat the completely novel radiation sickness is both inspirational and numbing. Dr. Hachiya was so severely injured that he had little opportunity to observe the state of the city immediately after the explosion. In the following selections from his diary three men describe to him what they saw as they struggled through the burning city to get to the hospital.

---

* These figures are from an American source. Japanese estimates run as high as 200,000 deaths.

MICHIHIKO HACHIYA,
Hiroshima Diary,
pp. 14–15, 19–20

"Let me tell you, if I can, what happened. Somebody told me that a special, new bomb was dropped near the Gokoku Shrine.* If what I was told is true, then that bomb must have had terrific power, for from the Gokoku Shrine clean out to the Red Cross Hospital† everything is completely destroyed. The Red Cross Hospital, though badly damaged, was spared, and beyond, going towards Ujina the damage is slight.

"I stopped by the Red Cross Hospital on my way here. It is swamped with patients, and outside the dead and dying are lined up on either side of the street as far east as the Miyuki Bridge.

"Between the Red Cross Hospital and the center of the city I saw nothing that wasn't burned to a crisp. Streetcars were standing at Kawaya-cho and Kamiya-cho and inside were dozens of bodies, blackened beyond recognition. I saw fire reservoirs filled to the brim with dead people who looked as though they had been boiled alive. In one reservoir I saw a man, horribly burned, crouching beside another man who was dead. He was drinking blood-stained water out of the reservoir. Even if I had tried to stop him, it wouldn't have done any good; he was completely out of his head. In one reservoir there were so many dead people there wasn't enough room for them to fall over. They must have died sitting in the water.

"Even the swimming pool at the Prefectural First

---

* A shrine near the southern border of the Hiroshima Military Barracks in the center of the city and less than 200 meters from the hypocenter of the atom bomb explosion. As the name of the shrine implies, it is dedicated to the defense of the fatherland.

† One of the modern hospitals in Hiroshima, opened around 1940, capacity 400 patients, it was badly damaged and many of its doctors and patients killed although fully 1500 meters from the hypocenter.

Middle School is filled with dead people. They must have suffocated while they sat in the water trying to escape the fire because they didn't appear to be burned."

Dr. Hanaoka cleared his throat, and after a moment continued: "Dr. Hachiya, that pool wasn't big enough to accommodate everybody who tried to get in it. You could tell that by looking around the sides. I don't know how many were caught by death with their heads hanging over the edge. In one pool I saw some people who were still alive, sitting in the water with dead all around them. They were too weak to get out. People were trying to help them, but I am sure they must have died. I apologize for telling you these things, but they are true. I don't see how anyone got out alive."

"Don't go," I said. "Please tell us more of what occurred yesterday."

"It was a horrible sight," said Dr. Tabuchi. "Hundreds of injured people who were trying to escape to the hills passed our house. The sight of them was almost unbearable. Their faces and hands were burnt and swollen; and great sheets of skin had peeled away from their tissues to hang down like rags on a scarecrow. They moved like a line of ants. All through the night, they went past our house, but this morning they had stopped. I found them lying on both sides of the road so thick that it was impossible to pass without stepping on them."

Mr. Katsutani paused for a moment to catch his breath and went on: "I *really* walked along the railroad tracks to get here, but even they were littered with electric wires and broken railway cars, and the dead and wounded lay everywhere. When I reached the bridge, I saw a dreadful thing. It was unbelievable. There was a man, stone dead, sitting on his bicycle as it leaned against the bridge railing. It is hard to believe that such a thing could happen!"

He repeated himself two or three times as if to convince himself that what he said was true and then continued: "It seems that most of the dead people were either on the bridge or beneath it. You could tell that many had gone down to the river to get a drink of water and had died where they lay. I saw a few live people still in the water, knocking against the dead as they floated down the river. There must have been hundreds and thousands who fled to the river to escape the fire and then drowned.

"The sight of the soldiers, though, was more dreadful than the dead people floating down the river. I came onto I don't know how many, burned from the hips up; and where the skin had peeled, their flesh was wet and mushy. They must have been wearing their military caps because the black hair on top of their heads was not burned. It made them look like they were wearing black lacquer bowls.

"And they had no faces! Their eyes, noses and mouths had been burned away, and it looked like their ears had melted off. It was hard to tell front from back. One soldier, whose features had been destroyed and was left with his white teeth sticking out, asked me for some water, but I didn't have any. I clasped my hands and prayed for him. He didn't say anything more. His plea for water must have been his last words. The way they were burned, I wonder if they didn't have their coats off when the bomb exploded."

Surrender

After the decision had been made to surrender it was deemed advisable for the emperor himself to inform the people. The emperor's brief radio message of August 15, 1945, was peculiarly dramatic, for the people of Japan had never before heard his voice. To the amazement of the Allied troops who had learned to expect suicide rather than surrender, the Japanese people were as obedient on this occasion as they had been when urged to prepare for death in the defense of their homeland. Mr. Aikawa describes the scene in the shattered remains of his school in Yokohama.

T. AIKAWA,
Hiroshima Diary,
pp. 108–109

At that time, our administration center was a classroom which had barely escaped the fire. The windows had no panes, and there were piles of embers and a crooked iron framework of rusty color outside. On that morning about ten students were working there, as the others were working in factories miles away. I usually went to the factory and the school in turn, but on this special day I went to the school. After a long talk with the President, we called the whole school family together in the courtyard to listen to the radio for the important news. The sun was burning just above us and the pavement under our feet was scorching hot, but in the dead silence of the heat we stood speechless, making a circle around the radio.

The time flowed very slowly and sometimes almost seemed to stop. I watched a drop of my sweat fall on the pavement and dry quickly. No sound, not even the rolling of a train reached our ears. The sky was deep blue, and there was not a plane to be seen. In the midst of a cloudless sky only the sun was awake.

Exactly at noon *"Kimigayo,"* our national anthem, came over the radio, then the excited voice of an announcer said:

"Now the Emperor will read a message on a very important matter."

This was repeated twice, and then there was a long silence. The silence, it seemed to us, continued for many minutes, and when expectation came to the bursting point, the well-known Imperial speech on the termination of the war began in the Emperor's soft but somewhat metallic voice.

"I, the Emperor of Japan and the Successor of the time-honored Imperial Throne, tell you, the subjects of this country. . . ."

The words and expression were very ancient and difficult, as were all the Imperial rescripts since the beginning of the modern age, but I could understand the meaning quite well. We had lost the war, and we had accepted unconditional surrender to the Allies, including the Soviets, who had so recently joined the battle against us. Everyone wept as the reading went on, and I could not restrain my falling tears. Tears fell on the pavement endlessly, then one of the teachers suddenly burst into loud crying. I said to myself, "Well, it is over—the long, long thing—the war—at last! How strange it is and how unbelievable it seems!"

PART VII. DEFEAT AND OCCUPATION
(1945–1952)

The Psychological Impact of Defeat

Crushing defeat in World War II left Japan an exhausted and shattered nation. Kyoto was the only city of any size not reduced to a smoldering ruin. In Tokyo alone more than 150,000 were killed in two massive fire bombings. Yet, because of the return of all Japanese from the forfeited overseas possessions, there were actually more people in the crowded home islands in 1946 than there had been in 1941.

The future in 1945 looked bleak, if not hopeless. The people had been led to expect the worst from the predominantly American occupying forces, a view supported by the emperor in his unprecedented radio message when he instructed the people to "bear the unbearable." Thus the Japanese were fully as surprised by the humane behavior of the occupying soldiers as the latter were at the docility of the Japanese.

The Allied occupation was to last nearly seven years. Though not technically so, it was, to all intents and purposes, an American affair with General Douglas MacArthur holding the position of supreme commander for the Allied powers (SCAP) through most of the period.

The major objectives of the occupation at the outset were demilitarization and democratization. The American plans envisioned an economically weak Japan, hopefully democratic, and definitely incapable of constituting a military threat at any time in the foreseeable future. Demilitarization was swiftly completed (there was little left to destroy) and major emphasis placed upon an incredibly ambitious program to remold Japanese society from top to bottom. The United States provided the food necessary to avert starvation; but no emphasis was at first placed upon economic recovery. However, as the cold war developed and the Chinese Communists swept the Nationalists off the Asian mainland, American policy on Japan's future role changed. A new ally was needed to take the place of the hoped-for United Nationalist China. Gradually in 1948 and much more rapidly after the outbreak of the Korean War in 1950, emphasis was placed upon the full economic recovery of Japan. The process of dismembering the giant economic combines was halted and labor unions, which had received vigorous encouragement earlier, were forced to tone down their demands. There was even a modest military buildup referred to as a "national police force." The American-inspired clause in the new constitution renouncing the maintenance of armed forces proved to be increasingly embarrassing to the United States government.

The meaning of the occupation experience for Japan's future is only beginning to be thoroughly assessed; but there is no doubt that the impact was both broad and deep. The following selection considers the psychological impact of defeat.

R. E. WARD,
in H. Passin, ed., *The United States and Japan*,
pp. 39–41

In a chronological sense, at least the foundations of an understanding of postwar Japan's relations with the United States are to be found in the fact of defeat. It was not so much the loss of life, the suffering, and the destruction. This was bad enough, but the country recovered quickly. By 1951, Japan was well on the road to complete rehabilitation, while by 1956 all major economic indicators (with the exception of exports) had surpassed prewar peaks. Far more important and durable were the effects of defeat on Japanese values.

This was the first serious military defeat that Japan had ever suffered, and the first time the main islands had actually been occupied by hostile invaders. Further more, it climaxed a period of almost fifteen years during which the government had tried systematically to imbue the Japanese people with a sense of national superiority and destiny, of ardent patriotism, and of unquestioning loyalty. No modern nation, save perhaps the United States, has ever been less prepared psychologically to face the facts of defeat and occupation. These were totally new experiences for which Japanese historical experience provided no guidelines.

Ostensibly, Japan adjusted readily. The population was remarkably docile and even cooperative. One strongly suspects, however, that a major reason for this was the shattering impact of defeat upon the values of the Japanese people. All of their prewar and wartime indoctrination was proved wrong, their sense of national pride and mission destroyed, their leadership and institutions discredited; and all they had to show for their loyalty and sacrifice was defeat and occupation at the national level and suffering and humiliation at the personal.

The consequences of this trauma are still operative. One sees them with particular clarity in the continuing bitter rejection of so many of the values with which pre-war Japan was most closely identified. A sort of pendular swing has been involved. Militarism has given way to pacificism, an aggressive foreign policy to an overly cautious one. Strong popular sentiments of loyalty to, and close identification with the regime on patriotic grounds are seldom encountered, and in their place one finds apathy, passivity, or rejection of positive identification with the nation or its political leadership. These attitudinal swings are complex, and it would be an exaggeration to attribute them solely to the effects of war and defeat. Yet war and defeat seem basic. They provided the disillusionment with the past, the personal sense of shock, and the national feeling that Japan must seek new values that underlay the success of the Occupation itself and many of the developments that have since taken place.

One so often has the feeling, where postwar Japan is concerned, that this is a people in search of unifying values. They seem spiritually adrift, their prewar identifications with the imperial institution and its semi-religious mystique, with the state and its mission, with community —and even with family—badly discredited and, for many, destroyed. Yet new spiritual moorings, although actively sought, have not been readily available. The popularity of the so-called "new religions" testify to the search, while the mounting delinquency and crime rates, the steady erosion of community and family solidarity, the increasing selfishness and amorality of interpersonal relationships, and the high absorption in private rather than public or community purposes attest its difficulty.

To be sure, the same could with some justice be said of many postwar societies, including our own. But there is an important difference. Before the war Japan was—at least with respect to values—a surprisingly solidary society. It is true that the particular value system involved was premodern and irrational in many respects and thus incongruous with the more modernized segments of the society. This doubtless made it more fragile and less able to withstand or adapt to the massive shocks of defeat, occupation, and accelerated modernization. In any event, defeat and its aftermath created a degree of dissatisfaction with the old value system and a comparable degree of spiritual drift that is impressive by any national standards.

This is a circumstance that must be taken into account when dealing with contemporary Japan. It explains a good deal of the opportunism and narrow absorption in national interests that characterize Japanese foreign policy. Larger viewpoints and commitments are apt to be a product of moral convictions of precisely the sort that postwar Japan seems as yet unable to produce. The opportunism and national self-absorption that one finds in their place sometimes verge on the narcissistic. . . .

There have been many defeated nations, but only one has been subject to atomic attack.

The frightful relevance of the destruction of Hiroshima and Nagasaki to man's future in the nuclear age keeps alive the memory of those August days among all thinking people—but especially, of course, in Japan.

The experience with the A-bombs has unquestionably contributed to the strong pacifist strain in postwar Japan which is clearly revealed in the support for the "no war" clause in the constitution and the refusal to allow nuclear weapons to be brought into any of the U.S. bases in the country. The organized opposition to nuclear weapons has been weakened by the emergence of independent, pro-Moscow, and pro-Peking factions. Nonetheless the general opposition to nuclear weapons and tests remains strong.

Though the bomb which fell on Nagasaki on August 9, 1945, was two or three times more powerful than the bomb that fell on Hiroshima,—days before, the hilly topography of the city prevented the destruction and loss of life from reaching the levels of Hiroshima. For this reason and the fact that it was hit first, Hiroshima is the city which invariably is first associated with nuclear warfare.

The Scope of Occupation Reforms

There have been many occupied nations in history, but the United States occupation of Japan was in many ways unusual.

———————

R. E. WARD,
in H. Passin, ed., *The United States and Japan*
pp. 34–35

This was no ordinary military occupation with goals limited largely to the spheres of disarmament and reparations. It was realized from the outset that an effective program of democratization involved far more than changes at the statutory and institutional level. And, as SCAP became more involved in the endeavor, its agenda of action tended continuously to expand. As a consequence SCAP at one time or another became heavily involved in: the purge of upwards of 200,000 individuals from public office or the possibility of acceding thereto; the writing of a completely new constitution; the drastic decentralization of what had been a highly centralized system of government; a complete reform of the entire national and local civil service; an attempt to establish a new democratic system of political parties and to regulate abuses associated therewith; the introduction of a completely new concept of civil rights, human rights, the rights of women, and the rights of labor; a complete overhaul of the judicial and legal system; a deliberate inversion of the theoretical position and powers of the Emperor; the dissolution of the system of giant cartels, known as the *zaibatsu;* the drastic reform of the land tenure system; the promotion of labor union organizations and collective bargaining; stringent control of credit and inflation; a total reform of the educational system from kindergarten through graduate school; an attempt to substitute the Latin alphabet for the traditional writing system; campaigns to eliminate tuberculosis and other epidemic diseases; and even an attempt to persuade the Japanese to give names to at least the main thoroughfares in their major cities. This is a highly selective list that could easily be multiplied many-fold. There were few aspects of the culture that SCAP did not in some degree become involved with. It was a saturation-type operation.

Considerations of this sort may also serve to place the Occupation as a whole in somewhat better historical perspective. One is dealing here not so much with an episode in military history as with one of man's most ambitious attempts at social engineering. What was being attempted was no less than the redirection along democratic lines of an entire nation's socio-political values, behavior, and institutions. That the society involved was both non-Western and traditionally authoritarian simply added greater challenge. It was planned—and hoped—from the outset that the "reforms" should have consequences that would far outlast the termination of the Occupation itself. It is therefore not surprising that Occupation-born issues continue to set an important part of the agenda of current United States-Japanese interaction.

The Impact of the Occupation on Japanese-American Relations

R. E. WARD,
in H. Passin, ed., *The United States and Japan*
pp. 54–56

As one looks back from our present vantage point over the events of the postwar period, it becomes apparent that many, if not most, of the salient characteristics of the present relationship between the two countries stem from decisions that were taken or circumstances that arose during the Occupation period. As has been pointed out, this is true of a large number of specific problems. Of much greater importance, however, is the fact that the basic style and context of postwar American-Japanese relations were set at that time. This is a fact of fundamental and continuing significance, and it may be well to conclude this chapter with a few words about why this is so.

The basic facts are simple:

1. The United States won the war; Japan was utterly defeated. The Japanese continue to be much more conscious of this fact and its many implications than we do.

2. The United States conducted a military occupation of Japan that lasted for almost seven years. Fortunately it was in general both humane and constructive. It was

also enormously ambitious. It set out to democratize Japan and in the attempt intervened in and altered in some degree almost every important aspect of the fabric of Japanese society. We then withdrew. The Japanese could not do likewise. They had to live with the consequences —good and bad—of our unprecedented experiment in social engineering. With some adaptations, they are still doing so. Again, they are far more conscious of this fact than are we, its authors.

3. The circumstances of both Japan and the world situation since the end of the Occupation have been such as to render Japan continuously dependent upon the United States in many important respects. This has meant that initiative and a wide range of controls have normally been available to the United States in dealing with Japan, whereas Japan's capacity to influence the United States' actions has been, while not negligible, relatively limited.

4. Japan would like to change this situation, but she presently lacks the viable alternative solutions to her economic and international problems that would give her the freedom to do so. . . .

One can also understand something of the psychological dimension of the relationship. At its core lie the elements of inequality and dependence. At every turn from 1945 to the present the Japanese have constantly found themselves in a posture of inequality and dependence. This is not the fault of either side. It is simply a product of the war, unequal resources, and a bipolar international situation. But it is a fact of which both parties cannot but be aware—the Japanese usually more than the Americans. A relationship so founded cannot be an easy one. The dependent partner is bound to do what he can to improve his circumstances. And this almost inevitably entails disadvantages to the other partner. Continuing elements of discord are thus built into the relationship.

Granted these elements of discord, however, the most important legacy of the Occupation is undoubtedly the continued closeness of the relationship between Japan and the United States. At any given moment the terms of this relationship are unsatisfactory to both partners. Japan would like to emphasize its economic aspects and to qualify a number of its military and political aspects. The United States would obviously like Japan to play a more positive and, we would say, a more responsible role in our global and Asian struggles to restrain the expansion of communist power. At present, and in the foreseeable future, there is small possibility of reaching a mutually acceptable accommodation between such discordant objectives, and the process of bargaining over the precise nature of mutual obligations at any given time is, therefore, certain to continue.

What it is important to remember is the considerable area of basic agreement that underlies this process of bargaining. However serious the disagreements about the strategy of dealing with the problems, no postwar Japanese government has favored what the communist powers stand for as opposed to what the United States stands for in international affairs. On balance, the contrary is the case. It is conceivable but improbable that this attitude will change in the near future. Similarly the United States, while bargaining for a whole array of more positive roles that it would like to see Japan play in the implementation of our foreign policy, can probably accommodate to a situation in which Japan would occupy a substantially more neutralist and disengaged position than she does at present. These probable outer limits to the two governments' perceptions of their national interests create a sizeable arena within which bargaining is possible as well as profitable for both sides. In this sense one can speak of a continuing, if shifting, congruence of national interests between the United States and Japan as the single most important legacy of the Occupation.

The 1947 Constitution

The present constitution of Japan, adopted in 1947, is based on a draft produced by occupation officials. If law could determine history there would be no reason to fear a return of authoritarian rule in Japan. The emperor is reduced to a "symbol of the State . . . deriving his power from the will of the people." The people exercise their will through the Diet which is "the highest organ of State power." At the personal instigation of General MacArthur there is even an article renouncing war and military forces altogether. Together with the provisions regarding the emperor this article is the subject of heated controversy in Japan today. Ironically, the pro-American Liberal-Democratic party favors constitutional revision, while the Socialists and Communists passionately defend the document as it stands.

A few articles from the chapter of "Rights and Duties of the People" serve to illustrate that the constitution is in some respects a description of what ideally *should be* rather than a readily enforceable set of laws. While the ideals behind the document are familiar to Americans, it will be a long time (if ever) before all of them are fully absorbed by the Japanese.

The opening of the preamble has a familiar ring. . . .

Text from *Facts About Japan,*
no. 81,

We, the Japanese people, acting through our duly elected representatives in the National Diet, determined that we shall secure for ourselves and our posterity the fruits of peaceful cooperation with all nations and the blessings of liberty throughout this land, and resolved that never again shall we be visited with the horrors of war through the action of government, do proclaim that sovereign power resides with the people and do firmly establish this Constitution. Government is a sacred trust of the people, the authority for which is derived from the people, the powers of which are exercised by the representatives of the people, and the benefits of which are enjoyed by the people. This is a universal principle of mankind upon which this Constitution is founded. . . .

Chapter II, Article 9. Aspiring sincerely to an international peace based on justice and order, the Japanese people forever renounce war as a sovereign right of the nation and the threat or use of force as means of settling international disputes.

In order to accomplish the aim of the preceding paragraph, land, sea, and air forces, as well as other war potential, will never be maintained. The right of belligerency of the state will not be recognized. . . .

Chapter III, Article 11. The people shall not be prevented from enjoying any of the fundamental human rights. These fundamental human rights guaranteed to the people by this Constitution shall be conferred upon the people of this and future generations as eternal and inviolate rights. . . .

Article 19. Freedom of thought and conscience shall not be violated. . . .

Article 23. Academic freedom is guaranteed. . . .

Article 24. Marriage shall be based only on the mutual consent of both sexes and it shall be maintained through mutual cooperation with equal rights of husband and wife as a basis. . . .

Article 25. All people shall have the right to maintain the minimum standards of wholesome and cultured living. . . .

Article 28. The right of workers to organize and to bargain and act collectively is guaranteed.

PART VIII. THE NEW JAPAN

Japanese Society Today

In April 1952 Japan became once again an independent nation. By the provisions of a security treaty signed at the same time as the peace treaty, Japan was closely allied with the United States. As tangible evidence of this link, American military men and bases have remained in Japan to the present.

Within the lifetime of an eighty-five-year-old citizen Japan had passed from feudalism through industrialization, military triumphs, shattering defeat, and an unprecedented effort by the victors to remake the nation. It is hardly surprising that major sources of tension should be found in contemporary Japanese society.

In a remarkable introduction to his survey of modern Japanese history the author of the following selection reveals through the description of a fictional Tokyo family a host of insights into the nature of Japanese society today. Although this book appeared in 1960, the rapid pace of change in Japan has made necessary editor's footnotes to update the description.

R. Storry,
A History of Modern Japan,
pp. 14–21

It is a winter's evening in Tokyo. In a four-roomed house in one of the western suburbs a family sit after supper catching what warmth they can from a charcoal fire,* known as a *kotatsu,* sunk in the centre of the floor. Over the shallow square pit that contains the glowing charcoal is a low table. Over the table is a large quilt, perhaps twice as large as the table. Round the table, sitting on cushions on the floor with their stockinged feet hanging into the pit and with the quilt covering their knees, sit four people of different ages. They are old Mrs Saito, her son, her daughter-in-law, and her eldest grandchild, a young man in his twenty-first year. This young man, Saito Mamoru, is lecturing his elders on the aims and ideals of the Chinese Communist Party—a theme on which he considers himself to be an expert, for he is one of the most active members of the Chinese Friendship Association at his university in Tokyo.

Old Mrs Saito understands little of what her grandson is saying—he uses the jargon of the Left intelligentsia and his speech is prickly with English and German words— but she senses that his remarks are both dangerous and wicked, and she becomes increasingly restive and disapproving. His father, Saito Terao, is more sympathetic, but as he dislikes seeing the old lady provoked he will soon take her side and tell his son to stop talking. This will be the cue for his mother, Saito Shizue, to act as peacemaker, to get up and fetch some bean cakes, or to suggest that they switch on the wireless. This is the crisis of the evening. The young man, Mamoru, will lose his temper and shout at his mother; whereupon his sister and younger brother, sitting just outside the circle, will look up—she from her film magazine and he from his school homework—and complain of the distracting noise. Everybody's face becomes suddenly red with embarrassment or anger. Grandmother says she will go to bed. Her daughter-in-law speculates aloud on the feelings of the neighbours. In the end, as on so many other evenings, Mamoru will apologize for his bad manners, but not for

---

* Now certain to be an electric heater except in some rural areas. [Ed.]

his opinions, and a rough kind of harmony will be restored in this overcrowded house until the next row. The Saitos are a typical urban Japanese middle-class family.

On the whole they are fortunate. Mr Saito has only a minor managerial position in the large company that employs him; but with the twice yearly bonuses he earns just enough to pay for his children's education. Things are not, of course, what they were before the war. In those days they had been able to employ a servant, a country girl who was happy to receive the equivalent of thirty shillings a month and her keep, with holidays twice a month and three days every New Year. Food, for the salaried man, was cheap in those days; and public transport was clean and not invariably overcrowded.

Still, life had been much worse at the end of the war and in the first two years following the surrender. After the incendiary bombs had burnt the house in Tokyo, with all its contents, to a heap of ashes and charred timber, the Saito family lived for weeks in an air-raid tunnel. Eventually, through the kindness of relatives, they found a plot of suburban land to rent; and on this they built, with borrowed money, their present home. When first built it consisted of one room only. Later, additions were made, thanks to a transaction on the black market in 1949. For Mr Saito, having some knowledge of English, secured employment during the early years of the Occupation with an organization closely allied with the American Quartermaster Corps. This stroke of luck was not the only one that came his way. Once the Korean War had started, the organization that employed Mr Saito began to make very large profits. Some of the benefits of these found their way to him; and when the Korean War boom ended in 1953, the organization had blossomed into a large company, somewhat in debt to the banks, but not over-worried on that score. Before the war the president of the company had been at the same college as the managing director of one of these banks and was related by marriage with two directors of another.

The troubles of the family, as Mr Saito would be the first

to admit, are spiritual rather than material. Mr Saito, if asked to explain, would put it this way.

Before the war, and during it, there was something to live for. There was, above all, something to die for. He never had much use for the old army. He had feared and disliked the military instructors of his school days, and his recollections of regular army officers were, on the whole, disagreeable. He had served his time in the army, in Manchuria and north China. He had not risen above the rank of Superior Private, and he recalled, with some bitterness, the bullies who had commanded his platoon and company. There were exceptions, of course. His battalion commander had been an admirable man, stern but not unjust, an inspired and inspiring officer. The regimental commander had been like god, as though sharing some of the holiness of the Sovereign whom he so devoutly represented and served. Nevertheless, as Mr Saito might reflect, that regimental commander, astride his horse reviewing his battalions in the dust outside some walled Chinese city, was as narrow-minded as the run of Japanese army officers, who, after all, had led the country into a disastrous war against the United States and Great Britain. Why fight both at the same time? Better to have concentrated on Britain first. Everybody knew that America was too strong. No; the old army was too like the old police force. You might respect them. Often you feared them. But below respect and fear there was, for an intelligent man, a very secret contempt.

And yet, this having been said, there was a certain spirit about the old days. All that talk about Japan's mission, about the emperor's unique position in the world, about the matchless virtues of the national morale—all that talk had a residual glory, for a Japanese, that no post-war disillusionment, however severe, could entirely shatter. It was a matter of ethics. Since the people knew that they were the twigs and branches of a mighty tree, whose trunk was the imperial family, it was natural for them to be honest and punctilious in their dealings with each other and in their mutual relationships within the family. Hardships could be endured in such a cause as the emperor's. And no corps of officers or police could stand between the love of the individual for his god-descended ruler.

Nowadays all that kind of thing had disappeared. Everybody was free, or claimed the right to be free. Schoolchildren knew little, sometimes nothing, of their country's history; and if they were aware that there was an emperor living in Tokyo they had no idea of his divine descent. Educational reforms under the Occupation and Left-wing teachers had overthrown the old, narrow, severe, but still (in Mr Saito's phrase) 'spiritual' school system in Japan. There was no moral instruction at school. No wonder then that, as they grew up, children were so rude to their elders, so selfish, so infected with Communist ideas. Things had come to a pretty pass when an eldest son could insult his own father to his face, or a daughter announce openly her intention to marry a man of her own choice, without reference to the plans made for her by the older members of her family.

Such thoughts disturb the soul of Mr Saito as he lies beside his wife on a thin mattress on the floor of the room in which, an hour before, the family has been wrangling.

In the next room the old woman turns her head uneasily on the old-fashioned wooden pillow to which she has been accustomed all her life. It is not the pillow that keeps her awake. Looking back on her youth she can remember no emotional friction as persistent as that which disturbs the family today. She blames her daughter-in-law for most of the trouble. When she thinks of the way she had to obey her own mother-in-law, old Mrs Saito cannot refrain from sighing at the easy life of younger married women in modern times. Old Mrs Saito no longer trembles at the recollection of that mother-in-law of sixty years ago. For through self-discipline she came in the end to be dutiful in heart as well as manner.

Her mother-in-law had been married when Japan was still feudal, with a Shogun in Yedo and the land divided among the *daimyo*. The emperor dwelt in Kyoto, secluded and holy. Her mother-in-law, who came from a family of minor *samurai* stock, had seen great lords arrive in Yedo borne in palanquins and surrounded by retainers carrying two swords. Although she came to accept the utility of such importations as banks, post offices, railways, telephones, and cameras, she never acquired familiarity with them. She remained until her death a figure from the Tokugawa age, as pliant and as tough as a bamboo in its maturity. She had died from a chill contracted at the Emperor Meiji's funeral. She and her daughter-in-law, already a widow, had sat that night near the Outer Moat, had pressed their foreheads against the cold pavement as the cortège passed, with its whine of flutes and creaking of ox-wagon wheels.

Old Mrs Saito well remembers that summer night in 1912. It seemed the end of old Japan. Three days later her mother-in-law was dead. Thank goodness, thinks Mrs Saito—as sleep closes upon her—the old lady never lived to endure the Great Earthquake eleven years later.

Young Saito Mamoru in the third room, in bed with his brother, listens with impatience to his grandmother's snores, loud through the paper screens. There is no virtue in these old people. They hate the new Japan. My father fawns on the Americans but in his heart he is repelled by the very thought of them. Yet he would sooner have them controlling Japan than see our country socialist. He would sooner have me a drunkard, sooner see me fritter away my life at pin-ball, than know that I have sympathies with the Communist Party. Why don't I leave home? But I can neither go nor stay. After all, it is terrible to be a Japanese.

Unable to sleep, Saito Mamoru switches on the electric light, hanging low above his mattress, and begins reading in a Left-Socialist magazine an account by one of his own professors of a recent visit to Peking. Probably he will never know that thirty years ago his father, too, had 'dangerous thoughts' and would read far into the night while the others slept. The books then were translations of Wells, Shaw, and Sorel.

In the Saito household there is a reflection of the tensions that afflict Japanese families today—the mutual opposition of half discredited tradition and iconoclastic experiment. Saito Mamoru and his sister, although they are hardly aware of it, are products of the American Occupation, Japan's fourth and latest cultural invasion, though not, surely, her last. The other three have left their traces in the Saito home.

Near the Shinto 'God-shelf', a small shrine on the wall above the sleeping figures of Mr and Mrs Saito, there is a miniature Buddhist temple, a reminder of the first cultural invasion of Japan in historical times, that of Buddhism from China in the sixth century A.D. In the cramped little kitchen there are the remains of a sponge-cake, a gift from one of Mr Saito's business friends. This type of cake, known as *kasutera*, was introduced to Japan by the Portuguese in the sixteenth century, together with Christianity. The latter the Japanese were to reject for more than two centuries; but they kept the cake. This second cultural invasion, which included some rudimentary but useful scientific knowledge acquired mainly from the Dutch, was not substantial, compared with the first and third, but it produced its own important reaction.

The third invasion, also from the West, began in the middle of the nineteenth century, soon after Japan was opened, at the point of the gun, to foreign commerce. It lasted with varying degrees of intensity until the outbreak of the Pacific War. Its manifestations in the Saito house are too numerous to be listed; they include, it might be said, every article of Western use in the home —from the electric light to the row of shoes and gumboots standing in the front porch, from the coathangers in the cupboard to the boy's bicycle pump near the kitchen door. The family do not have a flush lavatory, refrigerator, washing machine,* or fly screens on the windows, so it cannot be said that the fourth, American, invasion has made a material alteration to the house. But, as we have seen, its non-material effects have been considerable.

Inextricably mingled with these adaptations and borrowings from abroad are the traditional appurtenances of Japanese life: the straw *tatami* matting covering the floor; the wooden bath and the wooden tubs used in the bathroom; the rice container with its flat wooden server, like a sculptor's palette knife; the rope sandals in the lavatory; the *geta*, or clogs, by the front door; the quilts and sleeping garments; Mrs Saito's set of ceremonial tea utensils; the *kakemono*, the hanging scroll, in the recess of the main room; the *sake* (rice wine) bottles and cups; the kettle in the kitchen; and many other objects of humble and daily use. Most of them, it is true, derive from China or from Chinese influence. But they have become uniquely and traditionally Japanese.

The Shinto *kamidana*, the 'God-shelf', and the tiny Buddhist temple enshrine the spirits of the family ancestors; and even Mamoru sometimes prays briefly before them in the morning, though his prayer may be for a Communist Japan. When the old lady prays she is talking to her parents-in-law, to her mother-in-law especially, and to her husband, who died from a Russian bullet outside Port Arthur. But the *lares et penates* of the house include a wider company, a host of ancestors—warriors, merchants, farmers. Above and behind these are the greatest gods of all, the emperors, stretching back in line from the present ruler through Taisho and Meiji to the Sun Goddess. It is a proud, powerful, oppressive tradition, the finally inescapable legacy of long racial homogeneity, of rigid formalism and limited but incomparable art shattered time and again by the outrageous violence

---

* By 1969, 71 percent of all households had washing machines; 65 percent had refrigerators. [Ed.]

of man and nature. Such is the aura, intangible but omnipresent, imposed upon the Japanese by their history.

It can be argued that Commodore Perry, when he forced the gates of Japan in 1854, performed a prime disservice not only to Japan but also to the world. Pearl Harbour, one might claim, was the logical, indeed inevitable, delayed rejoinder to an unwanted intrusion by the West. The validity of this claim rests upon the nature of the Japanese race. Japan has been called, at different periods in modern times, the Britain and the Germany of the Far East. The Japanese have been described variously as quaint, brutal, sensitive, callous, refined, coarse, loyal, fickle, lovers of beauty, and creators of ugliness. Influences from China, Korea, Europe, and America have contributed their share to this contradictory amalgam. So that it is hard at times to isolate specifically native elements. Nevertheless the impact of something peculiarly Japanese, in art and war and commerce, has been a formidable phenomenon of the past eighty years. We have only to reflect upon such matters as *hara-kiri,* the tea ceremony, the Kamikaze planes, or the delicacies of Japanese painting. There may be stranger nations than Japan. But none, surely, in recent history has been so praised and so reviled, so much discussed, so little understood.

Current Problems: The Economy

The astonishingly rapid economic recovery of Japan after 1950 ranks with that of Germany as one of the "economic miracles" of the postwar era. Japan today is a vastly more prosperous and productive nation than she was in her best prewar years. Japan has led the world in shipbuilding since 1955, she is third in steel output, and second to the U.S. in the possession of electrical appliances on a per capita basis and in the production of automobiles. Only the U.S. and Israel have a higher proportion of young people in colleges and universities; Japanese infant mortality rates are below those in the United States. Average life expectancy is more than seventy years.

Yet there are economic problems to go along with the welcome statistics. In view of her near-total lack of industrial raw materials Japan has been forced to expend vast efforts to increase export trade to pay for the necessary imports. Japan's need for increased exports is forcing painful economic and social readjustments on the domestic scene.

Though Japan's economy has continued to grow at a rapid rate since this article was written (especially in such "advanced goods" as automobiles), the basic problems described below continue to confront the Japanese. Pressure from the United States and Europe for easier access to the massive Japanese market (both in goods and capital) has mounted. There is particular fear in Japan of an "invasion" of American capital, especially on the part of the burgeoning automobile industry. In this connection it is well for Americans to realize how difficult it is for another nation to be a "partner" of the United States. For instance, though Japan is now second to the U.S. in automobile production, her largest producer (Toyota) is one-twentieth the size of General Motors (in sales) and her largest steel company (Yawata) one-quarter the size of U.S. Steel.

PETER DRUCKER,
"Japan Tries for a Second Miracle,"
pp. 74–78

In 1961 the growth rate in Japan actually hit 15 per cent. The government, afraid of inflation, stepped on the brakes—hard—and forced a slowdown. But a Japanese "slowdown' would be a gallop anywhere else—the economy grew by 5 per cent in 1962 despite credit restrictions and officially decreed "austerity." (The U.S. growth *goal* is a rate of $3\frac{1}{2}$ to 4 per cent a year!) In 1959 the Japanese government predicted that the economy would double again in the ten years between 1960 and 1970.

Last September the Ministry of Finance cut the period back to seven years; the growth from 1960 to 1963 alone had already added 40 per cent to the 1959 economic level.

Japan, of course, has one very special advantage—a very low defense burden. Though growing steadily, the budget for the Japanese "Self-defense Forces" still takes less than 2 per cent of the country's national income—as against a defense burden of 10 per cent of national income in the U.S. (Japan and West Germany should be a convincing answer, by the way, to fears of the economic effects of disarmament.) But even after making full allowance for this and a great deal of luck, the Japanese economic achievement is still a real "economic miracle."

This sort of accomplishment ought to make the Japanese smug. On the contrary, they are deeply worried. A good many sane and unexcitable Japanese talk seriously today about what they call "a crisis of self-confidence." Why?

The immediate cause of Japan's jitters is that in her own self-interest she has to open her domestic market to competition from the West and especially from Europe and the United States. Since 1900 when Japan first began to export manufactured goods in quantity, she has been a tough, aggressive competitor in international markets. But her home market has always been insulated— and neither economically nor socially is Japan prepared for competition in it.

Japan is thoroughly mercantilist. It is, indeed, the one example of successful mercantilism which combines governmental direction with entrepreneurial vigor, and aggressive competition abroad with protectionism and imposed price stability at home. To do away with this protectionism at home is going to mean changing drastically both the entire system of industrial hiring and firing, and the long-entrenched but extremely expensive system of distributing goods.

Then why should Japan now, after her economic success, have to let the foreigners come into her domestic market?

Japan's entire postwar expansion has been in the new "advanced" industries—in machinery, synthetic fibers, and plastics; electronics, optics, and pharmaceuticals; trucks and household appliances. The "traditional" industries which dominated prewar Japan are no longer very important in the domestic economy today. Japan depends, for instance, less on cotton-mill employment than does our own Old South. But of her exports almost half are still in "traditional" goods—textiles, toys, footwear. On these exports depends Japan's ability to buy abroad the raw materials—above all, petroleum and iron ore—without which the "advanced" industries could not keep going for one day. And exports of "traditional" goods are shrinking—fast and inexorably. Japan is already outproduced and undersold in the "traditional" goods by such new, truly low-low-wage areas as Hong Kong, Singapore, the Philippines, or Pakistan. Within a very few years Japan will have to replace "traditional-goods" exports by "advanced-goods" exports. And the only possible buyers of these additional "advanced-goods" exports are the big markets of the European Common Market and of Great Britain, where Japan today sells practically nothing.

The problem of the "traditional" exports would have arisen anyhow—no one knew it better than the Japanese. The emergence of the European Common Market as a great economic power, however, brought it to a head a full decade before Japan was ready to face it. Suddenly last year, the Japanese realized—as we and the British did—that they must get into the European market fast or risk being out forever.

There is no economic reason why Japan's "advanced" products should not sell as well in Europe as they have been selling in the much tougher and much more competitive U.S. market. But the Japanese cannot even ask for access to Europe unless they offer the Europeans access on equal terms to their own lush domestic market of 95 million prosperous customers—which, after the U.S. and Western Europe, is the world's third-richest market. This, however, means that the Japanese for the first time will have to be able to meet industrial competition on their own home grounds.

To Westerners, who have been used to stories of "Japanese low costs," Japan would seem to have nothing to worry about. It is hard for us to believe, for instance, that Italian or Swiss silks could undersell the Japanese product. Yet Tokyo's largest silk store last summer offered beautiful European silks 30 per cent or so below the price of comparable Japanese fabrics, despite a fat Japanese customs duty on such imports. For Japan's is a high-cost economy, except in its most advanced industries, and especially in its advanced export industries. Labor costs run two or three times as high on almost any manufactured item as they do in the West. And the Japanese customer pays almost twice as much for distribution as we pay here despite our vast distances and high transportation costs. These are costs demanded by the social structure rather than by economic inefficiency and accordingly require social remedies with all their potential political dangers.

Let me explain. The Japanese worker is as productive as any worker in the world. He is better educated and better trained than almost any other worker, and he works cheerfully, hard, and for long hours. Yet, in some Japanese factories it takes six times as many employees to produce the same amount of the same goods as in a comparable American factory. The reason is Japan's traditional system of "lifetime employment" with layoffs or dismissals only for very serious misconduct. As a result most of Japanese industry is grossly overstaffed, and thousands of people for whom there are no jobs are kept on doing almost nothing in the plant or office. Very few Japanese employers know (just as very few American employers know) that it costs three to five times a man's salary to have him on a job—in supervision, in space, in paper work and record keeping, in heat and light, in materials, and so on.

"Lifetime employment," in turn, means that a Japanese over thirty as a rule cannot change jobs. He is paid by his age rather than by the demands of the job he performs. He is assigned, however, to a job on the basis of length of service. A new employee over thirty, therefore, could be given only beginner's work—and would get twice the starting wage. It is small wonder that no one will hire him. But then no one fires a man over thirty; the firm just keeps him on the payroll and invents work for him.

As a result, older industries and businesses bear the heaviest burden of overstaffing; and the coal mines and railroads, as they are everywhere else, are in the worst shape of all. New industries and new businesses also have high costs because an artificially created "labor shortage" steadily pushes up the wages that beginners can, and do, demand. Starting wages for school graduates have doubled in the last three years. . . .

But lifetime employment is much more than a matter of money. Until World War II it was almost entirely restricted to white-collar workers. Manual workers didn't achieve it until after the war and then only through bitter labor struggles. To them it represents, therefore, status and acceptance by society. An emotional issue anywhere (as witness our steel strike of 1959 over "featherbedding" or the long and bitter fight of the Flight Engineers), employment security is pure dynamite in Japan. The longest and most violent strike in Japanese labor history was settled only two years ago, after virtually a whole county had stayed out for eighteen bitter months in protest against a management decision to retire with a generous severance allowance two thousand coal miners in an exhausted pit. Yet, according to a recent government study, there are another 60,000 coal miners—one third of the total—for whom there is no real work, though they all have "full-time jobs."

The problem of distribution costs is just as serious, and it too is as much a social as an economic problem. The distributive system of Japan is essentially what it was a hundred years ago—it is still a multitude of small middlemen who live on a pittance but who when laid end to end represent a staggering waste. . . .

Yet these concrete social issues, as full of explosives as they are, frighten the Japanese less than the impact of foreign competition at home on their traditional mercantilism—which has all the force of an unwritten constitution. Opening the home market would surely upset the subtle three-way partnership among government, large business, and small business on which Japan's entire economic development has been based. It would force Japan to abandon the policy under which government prods industries to be productive and competitive for export, while it protects inefficiency on the home market. It would break up the peculiarly Japanese arrangement under which the large producers are hot and hard-hitting rivals yet maintain a price-umbrella for the small fellow. Above all it would force Japan to let the market decide what should be produced and how it should be priced—questions traditionally decided by political and national considerations. . . .

Unless Japan wants to choke off her economic growth and prosperity she will have to become an open competitive economy. But if she does, tremendous political pressures will build up that will challenge political courage, vision, and leadership.

The Current Political Scene

What is the political climate within which answers to pressing economic problems will have to be worked out? The basic lineup of the political parties is presented below.

LAWRENCE OLSON,
in H. Passin, ed., *The United States and Japan,*
pp. 57–65

Japan in the mid-1960s possessed remarkably stable political institutions that had evolved over a century of contact and interplay with the West. The public, enfranchised at age twenty, might not always vote in percentages the Japanese themselves considered desirable, but it took elections for granted as a part—albeit, perhaps, a less than vital part—of life, along with political parties, a national Diet and local elected assemblies, a trained bureaucracy, a system of courts, and the rule of law. Politics in their operation naturally retained a strong traditional flavor, but personal freedoms were protected by a very explicit Constitution; the press was free to the point of license, and religion was disestablished from the state. Political changes came about through elections, not *coups d'état.* Rascals needed not to be executed but could be voted out, and often were.

However, stable institutions did not mean there was no turbulence in the political climate. The people abhorred violence but were fed a steady diet of it in the public prints and, like any people, could sometimes be led into violent acts once their volatile depths were aroused. Within a framework of generally accepted institutions the conservative Japanese elite and the opposition faced each other, as they had ever since the end of the Second World War. In this "confrontation," as Japanese writers liked to call it, were found modern ideological elements as well as nuances of more personal contention in which one sometimes perceived echoes of the samurai vendetta of older times. At any rate, the confrontation conditioned all that Japan did at home and abroad in the political sphere, including its relations with the United States.

Defeat in the war did not produce a social revolution in Japan. The American Occupation authorities governed through the bureaucracy that they found intact, except, of course, for those who were purged in the early years. The conservative parties, reconstituted after the war, were descendants of prewar parties whose origins could be traced back to the early twentieth century and beyond. Many new faces were seen in politics, replacing those removed by war; the most powerful political leader of the first postwar decade, Yoshida Shigeru, was an ex-diplomat without political experience whose bureaucratic protégés were to be key leaders in party politics in the 1960s. But a number of prewar politicians survived the purges and were important in maintaining the continuity of conservative forces: men like Ōgata Taketora, Miki Bukichi, Ōno Bamboku, or Kōno Ichirō, who had come up through the party route before the war. One prewar politician, Hatoyama Ichirō, served as prime minister in the mid-1950s; and "pure" politicians contended for power with ex-bureaucrats in conservative party ranks.

The Liberal-Democratic Party, a union of conservatives formed in 1955, won every election, controlled the choice of prime ministers, and organized cabinets. It represented the conservative continuity, and its members, along with their peers in big business and the senior bureaucracy, comprised the civilian Japanese elite of the postwar era, when the old military elite had been discredited and abolished.

This elite was relatively small. It was not an aristocracy of birth, although studies (by James Abegglen together with Mannari Hiroshi) suggest that in postwar years the lineage of perhaps one-third of its members could be traced to the samurai class. Rather more crucial than birth was education. The sons of wealthy, well known families were likely to succeed, but their success was not assured unless accompanied by a measure of ability. With few exceptions, they had to take the same entrance examinations and ride the qualifying escalator with everyone else. A poor but bright student could gain access to the university if he and his parents sacrificed enough; and they often did, because a university education was the *sine qua non* for high responsibility, especially in big business and the bureaucracy. Graduates of a limited number of schools, the former Imperial universities plus a few others, monopolized the top positions in the elite. Graduates of Tokyo University (Tōdai) were especially numerous in the bureaucracy, but this was less true after the war than before. Tōdai graduates were also found in the key positions in Prime Minister Satō's cabinet in June 1965: he himself, his foreign minister, and his finance minister were Tōdai men. Moreover, they were able Tōdai men, who had shown personal excellence: in performance and loyalty, two primary values of this elite, their records were beyond question.

The men, then, with whom most Americans dealt, officially or unofficially, were a well-educated, hard-driving lot. By 1965, top leadership in business, government, politics and other fields was still in the hands of men born and raised before the war. Highly secular, their ethic was often described as "situational," or, in more pejorative terms, opportunistic. They combined a respect for order, harmony, and decorum in personal relations with an intense desire to acquire for their country and themselves the latest benefits of Western science and technology. Committed to an almost pathetic extent to the idea of material progress, in their public lives these men had one overruling goal: to rebuild the Japanese economy and re-enter world society as a respected power; to "catch up with the West" was the watchword of their national planning.

These were the proprietors and managers, not so much of land as of business and industry. They were not a landed gentry in the European sense—postwar Japan had no such class—but rather were trained to have confidence in commercial ventures and encouraged to engage in productive enterprises; capitalist risk-takers, whose daring was somewhat mitigated by the knowledge that government itself would usually rescue losers if they were considered important enough, because it conceived the nation's interests to be closely linked with those of large entrepreneurs. Business, bureaucracy, and the politicians of the Liberal-Democratic Party were wound into one knotted skein of economic and political designs, and top leaders in all three fields were linked by many ties of intermarriage and reached decisions in diffuse, consensual ways.

Examples of the self-protective behavior of this elite were evident throughout the modern period, as in early 1965 when the government intervened to rescue with almost unlimited credit a large securities firm, which otherwise would have gone bankrupt and might have dragged down others with it. The government bureaucracy thus was paternalistic; it set perspectives for growth and intervened continually in an *ad hoc* manner to guide private business toward approved goals, which businessmen were then expected to follow for the good of all. The day-to-day operation of the economy was left to private initiative and not mismanaged by inexperienced bureaucrats. Mavericks were more numerous in business and politics than before the war, yet the notion persisted throughout the elite that the whole had an efficacy beyond the sum of its parts, and such a view left little room for "selfish" individualism.

The innovation of "responsible government" after the war drew the elite even closer together. Since to reach cabinet rank one had to be elected to the Diet, many ambitious bureaucrats who had developed sources of political support during their careers in government service "retired" into politics in their fifties; for years thereafter, as senior party men or cabinet ministers, they could maintain close influence over their former subordinates in the bureaucracy, while their heavy election expenses were supplied primarily by donations from businessmen.

It ought to be stressed that the elite was not a corrupt clique isolated from the mainstream of Japanese life. To be sure, conservative politicians did not have to be either liberal or democratic to join the Liberal-Democratic Party, they were guilty of their share of corrupt practices, and the party was insufficiently organized at the local level. But conservative Diet members, as individuals, had strong personal followings in their constituencies and responded to pressures from many interest groups therein. Far from living in European-style decadence and isolation in the capital, many of them were of a singularly parochial, uncosmopolitan variety, unversed in foreign languages or the niceties of foreign etiquette, but deeply integrated in Japanese society and wishing to be nothing else.

Nor could leading businessmen be said in any sense to comprise a *comprador* class who milked their own people for foreign gain. American businessmen had helped put Japan back into international competition after the war by licensing technology in a thousand ways and providing large amounts of capital and know-how. They had wide, often cordial ties with the Japanese business community; and they could testify eloquently to the stubborn economic provincialism and fierce protectionist tactics of Japanese bureaucrats, and the tendency of businessmen to hide behind the bureaucrats' rules and regulations to gain points *vis-à-vis* their foreign associates. The bureaucrats themselves were relatively honest and efficient, and Japan was one of the few places between the Mediterranean and the Pacific where accurate statistics could be obtained.

On the opposite side in the political wars stood the successors of organizations that had led a more or less fugitive existence and been harshly persecuted before 1945. The springs of acrimony in Japanese political life long pre-dated the cold war, and dark memories on both sides affected every decision and policy, especially in the field of foreign relations. The way many Japanese saw relations with America deeply reflected Japan's own prewar political history.

In the immediate postwar period anything seemed

possible in Japan, including ideal democracy and perfect peace. Early Occupation policy was devoted to such goals, and it encouraged the re-emergence of political groups that had been treated as subversive before the war. One of these groups was the Japan Communist Party, extant, off and on, since 1922, but illegal from 1922 to 1945. Much more significant were the socialists.

The Japan Socialist Party was a grab-bag of theoretical incongruities and rival cliques. Its origins could be traced to the late nineteenth century, when Japanese industry began to mature and a complex urban society took shape. Whereas in the first generation after the Meiji Restoration intellectuals and government leaders had tended to agree on their modernizing objectives, by the turn of the century phenomena of alienation familiar in Western industrial states had appeared, and took various ideological or attitudinal forms: Christianity, hedonism, liberal "humanism," Marxism, and other "isms" were seized upon by various intellectuals to serve as vehicles to symbolize their distaste for the excesses of Japanese industrial capitalism. Early socialist leaders were labor organizers, university intellectuals, or social workers in urban slums; under police repression many of them moved farther and farther leftward. Prewar Japan had a bloody labor history, with prolonged strikes in copper and coal mines, shipyards and factories, where working conditions were often appalling and gave ample point to Marx's descriptions of English mills. Out of the confrontation, often violent, between such early socialists and the police, spread over nearly half a century, developed a movement that was badly fragmented into factions along personal lines and divided doctrinally according to the method believed most efficacious to define and combat the hated "enemy."

As can be seen, many leftists came out of backgrounds very different from those of the elite. The educational level and social origins of many socialists were lower. Some of them, Christians as well as communists, achieved prominence through their work with the poor in the slums of Kōbe and Ōsaka: a visit to a Christian youth center in Konohana Ward on Ōsaka's waterfront might have revealed one type of local socialist leader. Others came from areas of western Japan such as Okayama Prefecture, where efforts had been made, especially after the First World War, to organize the tenant farmers. In 1965, Socialist Party leadership included two such Okayama men: Eda Saburō and Wada Hirō. Still others had worked to organize and "liberate" Japan's outcastes, the *eta*, found for the most part in the western part of the country; one leader of the extreme left wing of the Socialists after the war was himself a member of that outcaste group. A whole stable of intellectuals served as theoreticians for the "social movement," providing theory for labor leaders and politicians who for the most part had come up through the labor wars. The Socialist Party chairman in mid-1965 was a university graduate who began life as a charcoal-maker in remote northern Japan; others were ex-communists or "crypto-communists" who tended to accept Marxist objectives for society but denied the infallibility of the Kremlin; theirs was a Marxism of a peculiarly Japanese variety. They were fond of "struggles" and "united fronts for liberation," and ambiguous in their attitude toward the uses of the Diet. Others, Christians, Fabians, and the like, preferred to work through legal, parliamentary institutions to bring about the revolution they all desired, or professed to desire.

In the fresh political atmosphere of the immediate postwar period the great majority of the Japanese people continued to regard communism as an alien, perilous creed. But the Socialists, despite their inexperience with power and their rancorous internal disputes, were perceived by many to be a valid alternative to conservative orthodoxy, which lacked color, was linked with a discredited ideology, and, after all, might some day be voted out of power. Dividing and coalescing for many years, the Socialists seemed unable to unite; in 1951 they split wide open over the San Francisco Peace Treaty, which the left-wing Socialists refused to accept; but by the mid-1950s they had formed a single party. Its principal means of support was the large labor federation, *Sōhyō*, whose leaders were under the influence of Marxist intellectuals and who, in the 1960s, leaned toward Russia rather than Communist China and were wary of the pro-Chinese Japanese Communists. *Sōhyō* provided most of the funds for Socialist candidates, and a large percentage of the candidates themselves came from the ranks of *Sōhyō* affiliated unions. Indeed, many Socialist politicians complained bitterly that the party was a captive of *Sōhyō*, and until it could find a wider support would never reach power. Late in the 1950s one faction broke off from the Socialist mainstream and formed the non-Marxist Democratic-Socialist Party, with a more moderate position, and more modest sources of labor support.

These disputes were symptomatic of the Socialists' endemic problem: were they to become a "class" or a "mass" party? Some urged that the Party modernize itself, cease to rely on strikes and street demonstrations, and attempt to come to power through parliamentary means. But those who favored such a course had not entirely cast off their Marxism, and for both personal and doctrinal reasons these policies did not prevail. Thus the Japanese Socialists remained the despair of their European socialist colleagues and in a kind of archaic dawn, clinging to an ideology that was already bankrupt as a possibility in the West. Their vote in national elections rose slowly, and their seat strength in elected bodies increased; but their chances of taking power on the national level in the near future were dim.

The Socialist contest with the Liberal-Democrats was the stuff of which postwar Japanese politics was made. Ideological differences between the two sides might not have been irreconcilable given enough time and a depoliticization of the atmosphere. But distrust was deep, and the two sides stiffly faced each other, the "ins" per-

manently in and able to railroad their measures through
the Diet by sheer force of numbers; the "outs" always
out, frustrated, reduced to using physical force to ob-
struct parliamentary proceedings and often preferring to
take to the streets. Each side feared and hated the other
because of the past, but political discourse was vastly
more inflamed by the circumstances of the cold war. The
conservative elite chose close alliance with the United
States as the only way to restore Japan as a major nation
and, incidentally, to keep itself in power. This policy fit
the leaders' goals: strongly anti-communist and intensely
nationalistic, they wanted wealth and power for the
nation above all else. The Socialists, partly out of hatred
for the conservative continuity, partly from ideological
motives, partly from sheer loyalty to their past and the
need for a clear-cut position, stood against the American
alliance. They called for a nonaggression treaty signed
by Russia, Communist China, Japan, and the United
States to guarantee Japan's security, and advocated dis-
armed neutrality. Their appeals for Japan's noninvolve-
ment in America's battles in the cold war had a strong
nationalist attraction to a people sick of war and afraid
of the ugly past's returning.

Liberal-Democrats and Socialists occupied the broad
center of politics. There were, however, some minor
parties: the Communists, relatively insignificant but legal;
the Democratic-Socialists, who sought without much success to establish themselves as a moderate party; and
perhaps most interesting, the religious organization known
as Sōka Gakkai, or Value Creation Society, which in 1964
established a "party," the Kōmeitō, as its political front.

Sōka Gakkai was founded in the late 1920s by an obscure
schoolteacher, who protested against the suffocating
orthodoxy of his day by writing lengthy theses concerned
with the "scientific" search for happiness. These activities
eventually landed him in prison, where he died of mal-
nutrition in 1944, leaving a handful of disciples. His system, briefly, proposed that man's happiness was the goal

of creation and that this happiness was to be achieved not through the search for absolute ideals such as truth or through worship of a transcendental God, but by the adoption of proper value judgments—the "creation of value"—in the shifting situations of human experience. His system, as the writer has reported elsewhere, was "vitalistic, energy-inspiring, wholly this-worldly, and remarkably Japanese."

Sōka Gakkai was essentially a faith-healing cult which associated itself with the Nichiren Shō sect of Buddhism and became that sect's lay religious order. It was fortunate to find a new strong leader after the war who gave it a tight organization, said to be admired even by the Communist Party and extending down to cell-like units throughout the country. Meetings of local members were held in homes rather than temples; some observers saw in them resemblances to group psychotherapy in the West. Membership multiplied very rapidly in the 1950s, when the heavy migration of people out of agriculture to cities began; and Sōka Gakkai attracted many thousands of persons in the lower levels of the working class in Japan's sprawling cities: proprietors and workers in the service trades and in unorganized small industries, who felt benighted and left out of the economic advance of the "new middle class" of salaried men and white-collar workers. Like some other sects that flourished after the war, Sōka Gakkai was essentially a nativistic movement that sought for some reintegrative symbols to take the place of those discredited by Japan's defeat. In this case their saint, Nichiren, a thirteenth century Buddhist priest, was seen as a world savior. Many of their leaders were young men with ambition to rise through their society; they may have believed sincerely in Sōka Gakkai's doctrines but they also saw it as a channel of upward mobility in a country still dominated by old men. By the early 1960s membership was estimated at some 7 million persons, but accurate figures were impossible to obtain. Sōka Gakkai leaders in Tokyo claimed 10,000 American members, and they somewhat annoyed American base commanders by proselytizing servicemen, usually through their Japanese wives or mistresses. Temples were opened in Hawaii, Los Angeles, and elsewhere outside Japan.

Sōka Gakkai's political meaning was not clear, but it deserved close watching. By enforcing strict bloc voting in upper house elections it polled over 4 million votes in the national constituency in 1962 and over 5 million in 1965. By the latter date its party, Kōmeitō, had 20 out of 250 seats in the upper house, making it the third party, after Liberal-Democrats and Socialists; and it announced that it would run at least 30 candidates in the general election for the lower house, which would be held some time during 1966.

There was a good deal of evidence that voters voted for Kōmeitō because it was new and they were tired of all the established parties. Its platform stressed this new-ness, standing for such unexceptionable things as clean government and more responsibility for youth. Otherwise its program resembled that of the Socialists: peace, no constitutional revision, reduction or disbandment of the Self-Defense Forces. These were things calculated to win city votes especially, but the Kōmeitō was not in any doc-trinal sense a "left-wing" party but simply a populist one, and its existence drew voters away from both Socialists and conservatives. How long it would continue to grow was unpredictable. As the Party became more important the problem of reconciling its religious sponsorship with its need for secular goals might increase. There was some evidence that its leaders themselves were unsure what to do with the religious pressure group they controlled. Factionalism might infect it as it had all other parties. The groups on which it battened for support were prob-ably decreasing rather than increasing in absolute num-bers, but there were still plenty of people to convert. Few thought Kōmeitō would take over Japanese politics, and it had not yet changed the basic dimensions of the conservative-socialist confrontation. But it was being watched very closely by Americans and Japanese alike because it testified to the continued presence of irrational elements in Japanese society that yearned for some kind of native Japanese ideological expression not being satisfied by either major party.

Allied with Japan's conservatives, America could not expect to be loved by the Socialists, much less the Communists. The opposition, although itself deeply divided, would accuse the government at every step of subservience to the American lead. The conservatives for their part left much to be desired, but as a group they were not the reactionaries their opponents made them out to be; and capitalism, with all its defects, was the characteristic mode of modern Japanese development. Japanese society was slowly opening and becoming more free, and America was well-advised, if it valued Japan as a vital ally, to avoid embarrassing the conservative government, narrowing its range of manoeuver and perhaps adding to the influence of its less modern elements. For the government represented the Japanese majority and stood for most of the things America in the 1950s and 1960s wanted to see develop in Japan: stable institutions, a dynamic economy, and an increasingly open society located firmly outside the communist bloc.

Political Trends

Major issues in Japanese politics are discussed by America's best-known authority on Japan in this selection.

EDWIN O. REISCHAUER,
Beyond Vietnam,
pp. 119–129

Despite the many serious problems facing Japan, I believe there is good reason for optimism with regard both to its continuing prosperity and stability and to its continuing friendship with us. It is true that Japan balances somewhat precariously on a narrow geographic base and thus is very dependent on world trade. As we shall see, it is politically a deeply divided nation. In its frantic pace of economic growth, it has seriously slighted the public sector of the economy in the postwar era. Housing is most inadequate. The problems of urban crowding and pollution are particularly severe because of the huge numbers of people crammed into the narrow coastal plains of Japan. Urbanization, modernization, and affluence have brought the Japanese many of the social ills we have experienced recently. They have some juvenile delinquency, though not so much as we. The greater speed of change in Japan has made the gap in understanding and communication between generations even more severe than in the United States. There is also a strong feeling among Japanese that their democratic institutions are undermined by corruption and voter apathy. They feel a sense of a spiritual vacuum—a lack of a new national "value system" to replace that of the authoritarian and militaristic past.

These are all grave problems, but Japan is facing them honestly and with about the same degree of success as other advanced nations. In spite of the spiritual confusion and the vehemence of political debate, the Japanese are far more united on basic matters than they seem to realize. There is overwhelming support for a peaceful role for Japan in the world and for a just international order under the United Nations. There is equally strong support for the new Constitution and for its clear-cut parliamentary democracy and broad individual rights. Only a small fringe on the extreme left and an even smaller fringe on the extreme right can envision anything but a democratic form of government for Japan.

There are actually few places in the world where the economic and political prognosis looks more favorable. Japan lacks the deep democratic roots of the English-speaking countries and some North European lands, but after these, its democracy is as firmly founded as anywhere in the world, being at least as stable as that of Germany, France, or Italy. The only great threat to Japan would be a world holocaust or a major worldwide depression, but, if either of these occurred, we ourselves would have many other problems to worry about more serious than Japan's future.

Japan's continued friendship with us may be a matter of greater doubt. To understand this problem we might briefly review the recent history of domestic politics in Japan. The Japanese emerged from the Second World War a confused and deeply divided people. A conservative majority, however, has been in control of the government ever since 1948. It centers around the Liberal Democratic Party, the heir of the two major prewar parliamentary parties. The Liberal Democrats draw their chief voting strength from rural and small-town Japan and their prestige and power from their close association with big business and the bureaucracy.

In opposition stand the Marxist parties of the left. As the most daring and vocal opponents of the disastrous prewar course of the militarists, the Marxists emerged from Japan's defeat as seemingly the most obvious alternative to militarism. Throughout they have proclaimed themselves the champions of peace and are commonly called the "progressives." They draw their strength largely from organized labor and from the intellectual and white-collar residents of the cities, whom the Japanese call by a very appropriate English term they have coined —"salary man."

In theory, the leftist parties are for a socialized economy, but, because of Japan's great economic success, their demands are somewhat muted on that side. A much more central issue of political debate is the problem of Japan's defense alignment with the United States. According to the Marxists, "American imperialism" which they view as an inevitable product of our "capitalistic" society, is as great a problem to Japan and possibly a more pressing one than is its own "monopoly capitalism." They feel that the United States, driven by its "imperialistic" urges, is certain to clash with the Socialist "peace camp," meaning the Soviet Union and China. Hence the Security Treaty with the United States and the American bases in Japan, far from giving Japan security, actually threaten to embroil it in war. A neutralist Japan, even if virtually unarmed, would be safer, they feel, than one tied to the American war machine.

During the past two decades, Japanese politics have centered around this debate between neutralism and alignment with the United States. The huge demonstrations against the Security Treaty with the United States that swept Tokyo in the spring of 1960 were an outgrowth of it, though certain peripheral issues, such as constitutional procedures in parliament and fears that President Eisenhower's proposed visit would constitute foreign pressure on domestic policies, added fuel to the flames. The treaty as revised in 1960 put limitations on the use and the armament of our bases in Japan as well as a ten-year time limit, after which it could be repudiated by either side. We agreed neither to make major changes in armament in Japan (that is, to bring in nuclear weapons) nor to use the bases in direct military action elsewhere without "prior consultation" (meaning agreement) with the Japanese government. Thus the revised treaty was much more advantageous to the Japanese than the original treaty. The left, however, opposed it because the earlier treaty had been imposed on an occupied Japan, while the now independent Japanese government was fully responsible for the terms of the new treaty. The government won out in 1960, despite the massive popular protests. Ever since, opposition has aimed at 1970 as the year when the treaty can be denounced and the defense tie with the United States ended.

During the past twenty years the once large majority

of the conservative government party has slowly dwindled. On the average, the voters seem to be shifting from it to the opposition parties at the rate of about 1 or 2 per cent per year. This seems basically a sociological rather than a political change. It reflects the rapid urbanization of Japan, the decline of rural populations, the growth of the "salary man" sector of society, and the shift of workers from small-scale, family enterprises to large-scale industries. In the general election of January 1967, the opposition parties together polled a total of 46 per cent of the vote, the remainder going to the Liberal Democrats and a handful of independents, most of whom were also conservative. At this rate, the opposition vote may exceed the 50-per-cent mark by or before 1970.

These voting trends are interpreted by some as foretelling a sharp break in our relationship with Japan in the near future, but this is too hasty a judgment. It overlooks the fact that the opposition is itself seriously divided. On the one hand, two of the opposition parties are more centrist than leftist. The Democratic Socialist Party, which won 7.5 per cent of the votes in the last general election, is essentially a post-Marxian movement, much like the socialist parties of Europe, and is strongly committed to parliamentary democracy and opposed to Communism. The Kōmeitō, the political wing of the Sōka Gakkai religious movement, which won 5.5 per cent of the vote, has no clearly defined political position but probably leans more toward the conservative side than to the left. The real left itself is also divided into two parties—the Communists, who won 5 per cent of the vote, and the Socialists, who won 28 per cent but are themselves deeply divided between a left wing that is at present more friendly to Peking than are even the Communists and a right wing that tends toward the Democratic Socialist position. Thus the opposition is divided four ways, and it seems highly improbable that it could ever coalesce into less than two groups—one pro-Communist and the other anti-Communist.

Another factor is that, while the vote has been drifting leftward, public opinion in Japan has been drifting toward the center. The labor unions, which underlie both the Socialist and Democratic Socialist Parties, have definitely moved toward moderation—that is, away from political agitation over global issues and toward concentration on the immediate interests of workers. The centrist parties and even the more moderate supporters of the Socialists have also gravitated slowly toward a more tolerant stand on the defense alliance with the United States and thus closer to a consensus with the conservatives. Even if the conservatives should lose their parliamentary majority in future elections, the most likely outcome seems to me not a government led by the left but a coalition between the conservatives and the more moderate elements of the opposition or possibly a coalescence of these elements with the more moderate wing of the right into a new centrist party. Thus a sharp break in Japan's relations with the United States does not seem probable.

The debate in Japan over the pros and cons of the Security Treaty is not the only strain on relations between Japan and the United States. The presence of some 40,-000 American servicemen in our bases in Japan inevitably gives rise to a large number of local frictions. So also do the sound nuisance of our jet planes in a crowded country, the extension of runways in a land-hungry society, and the occasional crashes of our planes on Japanese homes.

More serious is our continued military occupation of the Ryukyu Islands, which before the war constituted the Japanese prefecture of Okinawa, named after the main island in the Ryukyus. Our extensive system of bases on Okinawa, unencumbered by the limitations placed on our bases in Japan, has become a major backup for our whole military posture in that part of the world. At the same time, however, foreign military rule over the 950,000 Okinawan Japanese more than two decades after the end of the war is a growing cause for irritation and concern even among conservative Japanese and is a dangerous focus for leftist opposition to the American alliance as the target date of 1970 approaches. We have recognized that "residual sovereignty" over Okinawa remains with Japan, meaning that the islands will "revert" to Japan when conditions in the Far East permit, but this promise is too vague to satisfy the immediate nationalistic feelings of Okinawans and Japanese.

Economic frictions have also loomed large in Japanese-American relations over the past fifteen years. There have been perennial disputes over salmon fisheries in the North Pacific, and the Japanese, depending as heavily as they do on the American market, are also extremely sensitive to any American resistance to Japanese imports. Despite our championing of freer worldwide trade, we have forced on the Japanese so-called "voluntary restrictions" that limit the volume of their exports to us in a wide range of items from textiles to baseball gloves. On the other side of the coin, American businessmen are very dissatisfied with the severe restraints that the Japanese government has maintained in one guise or another on American imports and also on the introduction of foreign capital into Japan. Not long ago the Japanese were so much aware of their economic dependence on our market that they liked to say that, when New York sneezed, Tokyo came down with pneumonia. In the past few years, as Japan has become economically stronger and more self-confident, these tensions have relaxed noticeably, but there still remains a handful of troublesome trade problems that serve as irritants in the huge and complex economic relationship between the two countries.

Our foreign policy toward Asia has also become an area of serious friction. While the Japanese government has always stayed close to American policy on China in the United Nations and gives full recognition to the Republic of China on Taiwan, the general public is extremely restive about Japan's relations with China. The Japanese feel that because of their geographic propinquity, their special cultural relations with China throughout history, and their need to trade with everyone, including their great Chinese neighbor, Japan has much greater reason to desire full and friendly relations with Peking than does the United States. At the same time, they feel that, because of Japan's close alignment with the United States, American obstinacy has stood in the way of better relations between Tokyo and Peking. They regard this as the steep price they pay for their relationship with us.

In actuality, however, Japan does have important relations with Communist China. It is, in fact, China's biggest trading partner, and there is probably a bigger flow of people, for cultural or trading purposes, between China and Japan than between China and any other country. Tokyo does not recognize Peking, but this is basically because it recognizes Chiang's government on Taiwan, with which it has close relations and a very large trade. Japan could not do what France did in forcing a break of relations with Taiwan in order to recognize Peking, because Japan has far more important relations with Taiwan, as well as with Communist China, than does France.

The native Taiwanese show very warm feelings toward their former colonial masters, which pleases the Japanese, and they return these feelings. They also are grateful to Chiang Kai-shek for his quick repatriation of the Japanese soldiers and civilians stranded in China at the end of the war, in contrast to the Soviet Union's long imprisonment and harsh treatment of the Japanese it captured. Some Japanese also look on a Taiwan free of Peking's control as in Japanese interests. Thus Japanese involvement in Taiwan makes their China problem somewhat analogous to our own. In any case, America has not really stood between Japan and Communist China, and the incompleteness of the relationship between the two is basically because of Peking's intransigence and Japan's interest in Taiwan. Still, among the general public, Japan's unsatisfactory relationship with Communist China is blamed principally on the United States and serves as a major strain in the relations between the two countries.

As we have seen, the Vietnam War has become another important point of stress. When it was escalated by our bombing of the North in February 1965 and our subsequent injection of large land armies into the South, the Japanese public responded explosively in fear and dismay. They thought that Washington had become dominated by unthinking militarists, as had Tokyo in the 1930's, and that we would inevitably go on to war with Communist China and that Japan would then become involved because of our bases there and in Okinawa. They felt that we had embarked on a hopeless war with Asian nationalism, as they had during the 1930's and 1940's in China. As a nation all but wiped out by our bombing two decades earlier, they also identified themselves with the Vietnamese who were being bombed rather than with us. There were probably also racial sympathies in this identification. The government throughout has expressed its "understanding" of the American position but, in view of the strength of public feeling, has said no more. Since the latter part of 1965, feelings about Vietnam have subsided somewhat or at least leveled off, for the dire predictions of war with China have not materialized, but, as I have noted earlier, a further major escalation of the war in Vietnam could possibly destroy the whole Japanese-American relationship.

An important strain of a more general nature is the discrepancy in size between the two countries. We face this problem everywhere in the world, even with our major European allies and our closet neighbor, Canada. We are more than eight times Japan's size in economic power, and this already great discrepancy has been magnified by history. We represent the alien culture that destroyed Japan's "happy" isolation a century ago and threatened it with economic, if not political, subjugation. In the recent war we defeated and virtually destroyed Japan and then proceeded to occupy it and dictate its policies for seven years. Since then we have been its overpowering "big brother," defending it, providing it with its biggest market and most important economic contacts, and dominating its cultural relations with the outside world. It is easy for us to wish to deal on a basis of absolute equality with the Japanese, but it is hard for them to feel fully equal to us. The ills of the world—even of Japan itself—can all too easily be blamed on us. There is likely to be a big chip on the Japanese shoulder against the United States, or, if not that, at least a certain wariness and distrust.

All this contributes to a broad streak of anti-Americanism in Japan, but this we find in one form or another all over the world. It is the price we pay for our size and importance. In Japan it has special cultural and historical overtones. Much of the left is by definition anti-American. Among older conservatives are found the people who most bitterly resent the American occupation, because under it many of them were deprived of their former wealth or power and some were imprisoned as war criminals. Resentment of our destruction of Japan during the war, even of the atomic bombings, is surprisingly mild, however. The Japanese accept the basic blame for the war.

Beneath the surface of anti-Americanism, moreover, there is an even broader stream of pro-Americanism. Most people personally are extremely friendly to Americans. There is a tacit assumption that high standards prevail in the United States. Even our critics feel that there is more point in leveling their barbs against us than against our opponents, because they assume that Americans are reasonable and likely to act on the basis of principle. The attribution of all the woes of the world to us is in a sense a flattering overestimation of our importance. At the grass-roots level, pro-Americanism runs strong. Everything American—from gadgets to styles and political institutions—is assumed to be better than elsewhere in the world. The common Japanese pays us the most straightforward compliment of all—imitation. Advertisers find it useful to claim popularity for their goods in New York but would hardly be inclined to claim popularity for them in Paris or London, much less in Peking or Moscow.

> The author foresees no major change in the defense relationship between Japan and the United States; but he stresses the danger of continued U.S. control of the island of Okinawa.

The [U.S.-Japan] Security Treaty is clearly of great benefit to Japan—even greater benefit than it is to the United States. This simple fact, I believe, is beginning to emerge in Japan, as more and more people come to accept it as "common sense." It seems very improbable to me that Japan will seek to break the treaty in 1970, even though the left will no doubt feel committed to putting on a determined demonstration of opposition at that time. It is my guess that the Security Treaty will continue in effect without major modification almost indefinitely, as probably was expected in 1960 when it was first negotiated.

Of course, the actual defense relationship between the two countries will go on changing, as it has in the past. The American military presence in Japan will continue its downward trend, as the Japanese assume most if not all of the immediate defense of the islands and their near sea and air approaches. The Japanese government has set as a target 2 per cent of GNP for defense, which seems to me quite realistic if the defense alliance with the United States continues.

Okinawa presents a more pressing problem. It is at present very important to the whole American military posture in East Asia and as such is of great value to

Japan's own security. A major share of the economy of the islands also depends on our defense expenditures there. At the same time, the nationalistic yearnings of the close to a million Japanese in the Ryukyus and the nationalistic response of their 100 million compatriots in the homeland cannot be ignored in this day and age. So large an "irredenta" inevitably joins the deep feelings of nationalism to the dogma of the left and the passions of anti-Americanism. This is a problem that should be solved quickly, before the crisis of 1970 draws additional fuel from it.

A way must be found to permit the "reversion" of Okinawa to Japan without seriously endangering the security interests of both Japan and the United States. While our extensive bases in Okinawa are deeply entangled in the lives of the local population, means can surely be found to divide the bases from political control. The distance between our somewhat restricted rights in our bases in Japan and our theoretically unencumbered rights in the Okinawa bases is not really very great, especially when one realizes that no major American military effort in the Korean-Chinese-Siberian area would really be possible without Japanese support or at least tacit cooperation. Surely a realistic compromise between the present status of the Okinawan bases and that of the bases in Japan, which would permit the reversion of the Ryukyus, can be reached before 1970—or at least a fixed date for such a solution. This is in a sense Priority Problem No. 1 between Japan and the United States. The two countries are just too important to each other to allow an issue of this sort to endanger their relationship.

The great debate in Japan over foreign policy, defense, and the American treaty will continue to bubble and boil for the next few years, but I feel reasonably sure of the outcome. We and the Japanese are as natural partners as the United States and Western Europe. Of course, there are greater language barriers and, more seriously, differing cultural backgrounds and contrasting historical experiences. We were the victors and they the vanquished in the Second World War. We are reacting—perhaps over-reacting—to the realization that our isolation in the past helped produce the world conditions that led to great and destructive wars. They are reacting—and again probably overreacting—to the realization that their own militarism and imperialism brought them to disaster. The world can look very different from these two contrasting historical vantage points.

Nonetheless, the mutual advantage of close friendship and the fundamental identity of American and Japanese interests in the rest of the world convince me that the United States and Japan will continue to build a relationship with each other much like that between the United States and the United Kingdom. We and the Japanese have the same basic hopes for a peaceful world of diverse but nonaggressive national units living under a rule of law, as symbolized by the United Nations. What we basically want in Asia is what the Japanese desire even more emphatically. We have the same interest in maximizing world trade, only this is of even greater importance to the Japanese than to us. We and they have much the same ideals of a free, democratic society at home. While there is considerable misunderstanding and occasional mistrust, our actual conflicts of interest—fishing rights, airplane routes, and controls over the import of goods and capital—constitute only a trifling fringe of problems in a huge and mutually beneficial relationship.

It is probable that the Japanese, resentful of the long period of actual and then seeming dominance of their foreign relations by the United States, will demand a truly "independent" foreign policy. This is entirely natural and desirable. Japan will be able to do much more of value in the world and to be of more help to us at the same time if she is an independent partner rather than a reluctant follower. We should have no worries about whatever ties she wishes to make with the Soviet Union or China. The inflexibility and suspicions of both, as Communist states, and the Soviet refusal even to consider the return of the southern Kuril Islands, which the Japanese feel are rightly theirs, will probably keep these relations less cordial than might be desirable in the interests of world peace.

Japan's independence of us in the rest of Asia may prove an asset rather than a liability. It will give Japan greater freedom to play the role of bridge between East and West that has already been mentioned. It also may prove a useful counterbalance to us. Our size and power make Asians nervous about us. The presence of a strong and influential Japan in the area may reduce these fears. Similarly, as Japan gains in influence, Asians may begin to worry about its dominance, at which point we become a useful offsetting influence to it. Japan and the United States can probably achieve much more for Asia as two independent forces than if they were united in a leader-follower relationship.

As I see it, the chief problem in American-Japanese relations is that we both tend to take each other too much for granted. The Japanese have assumed that no matter what they do we will continue to play the stabilizing military role in East Asia that we have in the past and also will continue to contribute to Asia's economic development. It has, therefore, seemed convenient to some Japanese to accept the benefits of the American policy while disassociating Japan from any of its costs or dangers. In a sense, these Japanese have wished to continue the international situation of the time of the American occupation, when all international responsibilities did fall on the United States and none on Japan.

We, for our part, have tended to overlook the great importance to us of what Japan is and what role it may play in Asia. While overreacting to very remote or indirect threats to our interests in China and the rest of Asia, we have been somewhat insensitive to how our reactions might affect Japan and our relations with it. Such considerations should be a major factor in determining our policies toward China or Vietnam, but they never have been. Our escalation of the war in Vietnam in 1965 so frightened the Japanese that it clearly delayed their emergence in a more positive role of economic aid and political involvement in Asia. This was detrimental both to our long-range interests and to theirs.

While Japan will continue to depend heavily on our military presence in the Western Pacific, the United States will increasingly depend on Japan's economic cooperation and on its political initiatives in the whole area. We and the Japanese in our own respective interests must consult with each other on major policy problems much more fully than we have in the past and must let our respective policies be more strongly influenced by the other's point of view. This is the only way that we can give each other the mutual support we both need.

We should also be sure that we are treating Japan as a full equal economically. Using the argument that Japanese wages are cheap—an argument that is, incidentally, no longer valid—we have, through "voluntary restrictions," created barriers to Japanese imports that we do not place in the way of trade with the other industrialized nations. Discrimination of this sort against any of the advanced industrialized countries and particularly against the one that diverges culturally from the others is very unwise.

Actually this problem concerns all the advanced industrialized countries. The future of Japan is proportionately as important to Australia, Canada, New Zealand, and the countries of Western Europe as to us. But they have tended to discriminate against it economically much more than we do. Barriers to Japanese imports, imposed when Japan was a defeated enemy, remain high in Europe. Australia and Canada, while finding a major market in Japan, keep imports from Japan to only a little over half of exports. Although we managed in 1964 to get membership for Japan as the one non-Atlantic member of the OECD (Organization for Economic Cooperation and Development), the economic club of the advanced nations, it has still not been given fully equal economic treatment by the others. Of course, the other side of the coin is that Japan itself should stop its special discriminatory practices against the goods and capital of the United States and the other advanced nations.

In their search for a world role and "national identity," some Japanese wonder if Japan is essentially "Asian" or "Western." If by "Western" they mean "modern," then the answer, of course, is that it is both. That is the true significance of Japan's position. It can play its bridge role only if both ends of the bridge are securely anchored. Its economic, intellectual, and cultural interests lie overwhelmingly in its relations with the advanced Western nations. The firmer that end of the bridge is, the better it will reach across to the other side, where emotion, history, and geographic propinquity pull the Japanese. There is talk in Japan of a Pacific Community consisting of Japan, the United States, Australia, Canada, New Zealand, and, in time those Asian countries that qualify economically for membership. Such an organization, I feel, would strengthen the "modern" end of the bridge and enhance rather than detract from Japan's role in regional Asian groupings.

In any case, major objectives of America's Asian policy should be to encourage the prosperity and stability of Japan, strengthen its ties of full equality with us and the other modernized countries of the West, and cooperate with it in its growing role of economic aid and bridge-building in Asia. These are all matters of crucial importance to us, for not only is Japan of great significance in itself but our future relationship with all the rest of Asia depends to a very large extent on what Japan becomes and what it does.

Foreign Relations: The Appeal of Neutralism

Despite her very great economic power Japan's voice in international affairs has been muted over the past decade. However, stirrings of a new nationalism are increasingly apparent. Supporters of both the conservative and progressive parties are beginning to demand that Japan speak up and take a more independent role. The criticism that Japan is too closely tied to U.S. apron strings is frequently heard.

The following selections by two Japanese commentators pinpoint the hottest issues in the current debate. The first selections are from an article by an assistant professor of the faculty of law at Kyoto University.

MASATAKA KOSAKA,
"A Japanese View of America,"
pp. 20, 24, 26, 28

A third of the Japanese regularly vote for the Socialist party, which has taken a stand in favor of neutralism. Their official statements seem to reflect only stale anti-Americanism based on dogmatic Marxism. The Socialists declare that the Security Treaty between Japan and the U.S. contributes to tension in the Far East and threatens the peace. Capitalist countries, they say, are warlike by their very nature.) But, in fact, the sentiments they mirror are more widespread and more basic. Intellectually as well as emotionally, the Japanese people tend to believe that neutralism will probably lead to peace and that the present Japan-U.S. Security Treaty is likely to perpetuate a dangerously tense situation in the Far East. Because most Americans regard neutralism as a passive —an escapist design for withdrawal from the world— they fail to understand that it represents a positive policy to many people in Japan. To them it means independence and greater freedom of action; it means possibly playing a forceful role in a world free from military entanglement.

Personally I do not believe that neutralism is a proper policy for Japan; the world is not as peaceful as some pacifists like to think, and what precarious peace exists is maintained by a balance of power between East and

West. But I do believe that Americans must come to appreciate the very real attractions of a neutralist stance.

Our basic attitude toward military problems is admittedly difficult for Americans to grasp because it is so different from yours. Americans appear to think that the greater the military force, the greater the deterrent. We don't agree. Armaments to us are necessary but dangerous, and we believe in keeping them to an absolute minimum. Many Japanese, including those who support the alliance with the United States, think that the American forces in the Far East are too strong for purely defensive purposes.

Moreover, as we see it, the role of armed forces is slowly decreasing today. Of course, there are bitter struggles going on in Southeast Asia. But the fact that these struggles cannot be won by military power alone is apparent from the experience in Vietnam. In today's world, a contingent of Peace Corpsmen is, in a sense, more powerful than a Polaris submarine. Similarly, business negotiations and academic conferences may have more long-run significance than consultations among military leaders. We are willing enough to cooperate with the United States in strengthening the Free World, but we wish to do so mainly on an economic and cultural level. . . .

I urge the abolition of American military bases in Japan except where they are absolutely necessary. I cannot see why, for example, American air forces could not be removed. The Seventh Fleet, constantly cruising the Pacific, is strong enough to defend the Far East and to deter any full-scale Communist aggression. In an emergency, American air forces could surely arrange to use Japanese bases as well as the vital and imposing U.S. bases in Okinawa.

The Okinawan bases present another obstacle to Japanese-American friendship. America seems not to know or not to care about the Okinawan people but, to the Japanese their plight is heartrending. Okinawa has been torn from Japan but does not really belong to anyone. The United States, while admitting that Japan has sovereignty, continues to assert a right of temporary control over the island. A few years ago a visiting American scholar boasted in a lecture that the United States had taken no territory from Japan, while the Soviet Union had grabbed the Kuril Islands. A friend of mine, who is no anti-American, retorted by saying, "Yes, the Russians took the Kurils, but they are at least honest enough to admit it. The United States took Okinawa, but it's sufficiently hypocritical to deny it." . . .

Foreign Relations: A New Role for Japan

An adviser and former chief editorial writer of one of Japan's major daily newspapers pursues the issue of a new role for Japan in international affairs.

———————

SHINTARO RYU,
"Resetting the Course,"
pp. 43–45

Just as it is unreasonable to pin too great hopes on, say, economic relations with Communist China, so it is a mistake to fear her excessively. Nonetheless, it is a natural human desire in a neighboring country to wish to establish normal relations with her. It is perfectly natural that the Japanese should feel somehow unsettled until they have done so. China, admittedly, shares with America and the Soviet Union the advantage over Japan of being a large country—though until only twenty years ago, in fact, this vast size was a source of all kinds of hardships for her. As in physics, it is human nature to be attracted toward what is large. Moreover, China and Japan share common cultural ground, including even the same script, and Japan has become sufficiently strong to dispel the fear that Chinese communism could cause ideological disruption. The desire of the Japanese for natural relations with China has fully matured by now. It follows that, if Communist China should be admitted to the United Nations, Japan would automatically decide to recognize her.

The reason why Japan cannot do this immediately is, of course, her relations with Taiwan. This problem, frankly, is too great for Japan to deal with by herself. The fact that America is still more deeply involved in the problem is, for Japan, both an advantage and a disadvantage. Even should some acceptable solution be forthcoming in Japan, Japan would be powerless to make Taiwan accept it. As I see it, only America can assign Taiwan some appropriate and viable standing in the world and get her to accept it. The U.S. and Japan should join hands in seeking some solution of the problem.

Of late, Japan's relations with the Soviet Union have been sunny and unruffled on the surface. Yet the all-important Soviet-Japanese peace treaty remains unsigned, for the sole reason that the ownership of one part of the Kuriles cannot be decided. Some settlement must be achieved as soon as possible here. Personally, I believe the proper time to do so would be, as I shall discuss later, the occasion of the next revision of the Security Treaty between the United States and Japan. If at that time the few U.S. bases remaining in Japan could be removed, this would be an ideal chance to press the Soviet Union for concessions on its side. Either way, the establishment of a completely peaceful relationship between Japan and the Soviet Union is an urgent necessity. No good can come of leaving the question to take care of itself as at present.

As the preceding three sections will have suggested, the American influence on Japan is in fact a product not merely of U.S. policies toward Japan as such, but also of her world policies toward Communist China,

Taiwan, and elsewhere, which have direct repercussions in Japan.

Be that as it may, almost all the difficulties in Japan's international relationships have some bearing on her relationship with the United States. And the question is complicated still further by the fact that Japan is indebted in extremely large measure to America for her present situation, and that America must accept much of the responsibility for it.

The past, however, is the past; the question today is for Japan to extricate herself from her present contradictory position and get back on the right course. And this, again, can only be achieved through the best kind of relationship with America. . . . Granted that in this new situation continued efforts are to be made to achieve an adjustment of relations with Communist China and the Soviet Union, then it follows that the time has come for a reappraisal of the Security Treaty also.

It goes without saying that such changes in treaties should be undertaken with the utmost caution. One thing I do feel, however, is that Japan can have no obligation to go along with America in the cold war any further, and that she should concentrate on extricating herself from it as gracefully as possible. . . .

It seems to me that in an increasing number of cases new alliances today actually give less guarantees of security if they extend to military matters. It would be difficult otherwise to account for the number of countries nowadays who believe in non-alignment. I would propose, therefore, that Japan and America should reach some agreement in which economic and spiritual—chiefly cultural—relations would play the main part, and under which American forces would not be stationed on Japanese soil, America merely keeping a friendly eye on Japan's security.

I believe that this would create between Japan and America a type of international relationship hitherto unknown in history, one that would serve as a model for international relationships in the future. Everything that jars in the relationship at the moment derives from the existence in Japan of bases which are, in fact, of little value to the American forces themselves. The almost daily demonstrations by students now in progress against the entry into Japanese harbors of a single nuclear submarine not even carrying nuclear weapons are in no sense a sign of stupidity on the part of the students. If only America would show a wiser attitude in dealing with this type of question, there is no doubt that the feelings of the entire Japanese people would undergo a great change.

The Future

These selections are from an essay in which an American specialist on Japanese affairs presents a carefully reasoned prediction of major developments in Japan over the next decade—in economic affairs and in the area of international relations.

HERBERT PASSIN,
The United States and Japan,
pp. 144–147, 153–156, 158–161

By 1975, Japan is expected to have a population fairly stabilized at about 108.6 million. Her GNP will more than double and her per capita GNP will rise from about $600 per year (in 1965) to the neighborhood of $1,500 per year. As the world's third industrial power, she will have a highly developed production capacity, able to compete with others even in the most sophisticated hardware. She is likely to have a moderate missile-delivery capacity, as a result of her rocket research, even though she will not have made the decision in favor of a nuclear force.

This growth will be accompanied by drastic structural changes, essentially toward higher technological levels.

. . . Japan's agriculture, by 1975, will show a rather different pattern of production from the traditional one, with lesser dependence on rice, and a much higher ratio of high-quality specialty farming, such as dairying, livestock, fruits, and vegetables. . . .

This means that the villages, the bastions of Japan's "traditional culture," will wither away rapidly, declining to an estimated 18 per cent of the population. New forms of urban life, with its attendant problems, will expand. The urban population will increase rapidly, and several cities will advance toward megalopolitan proportions. Because of the space shortage and the high price of land, a decisive shift will have been made from the traditional pattern of single-family dwellings to apartment-style living. More and more Japanese will live in small, crowded quarters in multi-story buildings and, because of the high level of material prosperity, these quarters will be crammed with radios, color television sets, refrigerators, room coolers, air conditioners, and washing machines. Labor-saving (but space-filling) gadgets will reduce free space to a caricature of the traditional uncluttered Japanese house. Family problems will increase, what with the difficulty of supervising children at play in the streets, the scarcity of room for elders, and the loss of space for privacy.

The labor force in 1975 will be a very high quality one, both in terms of skill and educational level. By 1975, at least 80 per cent of young people can be expected to go through senior high school, and at least 25 per cent to go on to some form of college-level education. White-collar labor will increase enormously, as the proportion and perhaps even the absolute numbers of blue-collar workers decline. A white-collar style characterized by long commuting and relative isolation of family units, will become the predominant mode of urban life. Private automobile ownership, although not reaching American dimensions, will advance from its present 16 per thousand to something on the order of 35 per thousand, that is, approximately to present-day Western European proportions. Despite a vast road-building program, the gap between the number of cars and the roadways to carry them will continue to increase.

Welfare-state measures will expand modestly in such fields as medical care, old-age pensions, and aid to depressed areas and groups, and spectacularly in the case of education. The "leisure boom," already well under way in the late 1950s and early 1960s, will go on to new heights. Vacations will reach European proportions, with more people having longer holidays that will have to be filled by the expanding leisure-related industries. . . .

The process [of increasing consumption] can be expected to bring innumerable problems and frustrations. The dislocation and mobility of vast rural populations, the difficult adaptations to urban life, the loss of supporting community and family institutions, the periodic inflation, the unevenness of advance in various sectors, the sharp short-term ups-and-downs, the inability of housing and amenities to keep up with urban growth, the crowding of schools, transportation, and other facilities—all of these will combine to keep aspiration and opportunity continuously out of balance. All of the people will be frustrated some of the time, and some of the people will be frustrated all of the time.

We cannot anticipate how much expansion there will be in foreign trade nor how large the shifts will be, but the general lines seem to be clearly marked out. Japan should end up in 1975 somewhat less dependent on the American relationship than during the first two postwar decades. . . . In place of the United States, Japan will find markets and sources in some of the outlying developed countries, such as Australia and Canada, although the level of trade with Europe does not seem likely to rise very much. We may expect a steady increase in trade with China, even though it may not reach the proportions predicted by some wishful thinkers. As for the U.S.S.R., the volume of increase is likely to be more modest, unless proposed Japanese participation in the development of Siberia reaches significant proportions. Assuming that Southeast Asia does not go completely under communist control, Japan's involvement in that area is likely to increase enormously; perhaps the main limitation will be the area's capacity to generate purchasing power to buy in Japan. The proportional increase of trade relations with the Eastern European bloc should be considerable, although the absolute amount is likely to remain modest during this period. Among the underdeveloped countries, the most promising area for fairly rapid expansion is Latin America, although modest absolute increases in Africa and the Middle East may also be expected.

There are several constants that seem likely to condition the shape of Japan's internal politics throughout the decade. First, is the growing nationalism. We can expect Gaullist France to exert great fascination on both conservatives and progressives, and even though a Japanese de Gaulle is unlikely there will be growing support for a Japanese version of Gaullism without de Gaulle.

Throughout the period, Japan will probably remain disproportionately weak as a military power, even though there may be some modest increase in the size of her Self-Defense Force. . . .

Another factor likely to remain constant is the attractiveness of Marxist rhetoric to the educated classes. We can expect the word "socialism" to retain its favorable aura of purity and civic virtue to large numbers of people, and "progressive" will continue to sound more attractive than "conservative." . . .

The first general problem has to do with Japan's role in world affairs. That this will be fairly considerable cannot be doubted. Japan will play an increasingly important role in U.N. affairs, the settlement of disputes around the world, economic and technical aid, and international trade. But there will still be important constraints on her actions.

The first of these will be the predispositions the Japanese are likely to carry into the decade 1965–75, the ways in which they are likely to perceive the outside world. Perhaps the most important is their steady disinclination to accept the American view of global struggles. Communism and nationalism must go through a natural cycle of their own, and they cannot safely be stopped in midstream. This implies not only a policy of live and let live, but of avoiding commitment on the one hand and of trying to be friendly with everybody on the other. . . .

Therefore, Japanese are not deeply disturbed by the prospects of communist expansion. If it is inevitable, whether one likes it or not, there is no use resisting it; the greater part of wisdom is to learn how to get along with it. . . .

It follows, therefore, that Japanese in general do not feel themselves facing an external military threat. Partly this feeling of security comes from the absence of land borders—an island country enjoys a considerable immunity against land invasion—partly from the estimate that China, in spite of appearances, is not really aggressive. . . . The main danger of war comes from involvement in American actions based on the home islands or Okinawa, which can expose Japan to retaliation. It is clear that many Japanese will feel that remilitarization, the reemergence of the military as a political force, and the revision of the Constitution are more urgent problems than defense against a non-existent external military threat.

But if this is a widespread mood it is by no means universal. In the first place, there are many, and possibly even a majority, who disagree with all or some of it. Japan, they would hold, as an advanced industrial democracy, belongs naturally in the free world camp. . . .

Internal disunity, therefore, is likely to remain one of the important constraints on Japan's international role. Even if a national consensus continues to expand, it will be one of mood rather than of political particulars. The

divisions will remain too deep to permit the crystalliza-
tion of a genuine political consensus. Japan's ability to
act, particularly on internally divisive issues, will be
severely inhibited.

The most important diplomatic development will be
the recognition of Communist China. The timing and the
form cannot be fully anticipated, but the fact itself cannot
be doubted. Relations with China have become the symbol *par excellence* of Japanese "subservience" to the
United States, so that any government will have to come
to terms with the problem. By the mid-1960s it was already
quite clear that a majority of articulate opinion favored
official recognition of the Mainland. . . .

Relations with other communist countries can also be
expected to expand, although not to the same extent or
with the same emotion as in the case of China. A Japa-
nese-Soviet peace treaty, formally ending the state of
war, is likely. But frictions over fisheries rights in the
North Pacific and over the territories taken during the
war can be expected to continue. Japanese participation
in Siberian development may come to be a major element on the scene in the 1970s. . . .

An independent Japan will have to deal more seriously
with her defense problems. By the mid-1960s it had still
been possible for the general public to hold aloof and
to see the current stage of minimal rearmament as part
of the price of dependence on the United States. There
are good chances, however, that the entire context of the
problem may shift. Once the United States has with-
drawn, and even perhaps given up Okinawa for more
distant bases in the Philippines, Guam, and Hawaii,
Japan will be exposed to new pressures that she will have
to face up to. The confrontation with China will undoubtedly stir support for a larger defense establishment
and perhaps even a nuclear capacity. . . .

But the counter-forces of pacifism, fear of military re-
vival, and support of the Constitution will also remain
strong. Strong enough, at any rate, to hamper what

Americans would regard as a realistic reconsideration of the defense issue. The argument will be effectively made that a relatively unarmed Japan is more acceptable throughout the world than a heavily-armed Japan that revives memories of the imperialist past. There will also be fears about the effects of serious rearmament on economic growth. . . . Because public sentiment will continue to make any form of rearmament, and especially nuclear rearmament, very difficult, Japan may end up in the 1970s in a curiously paradoxical position. While most aspiring nuclear powers can be expected to develop some nuclear capacity and only reach delivery capacity much later, Japan may reverse this order of events. As a result of her advanced rocket research, Japan may have a potentially operational delivery system ready well before she has developed nuclear capacity. . . .

We can expect a continuing disposition to demand greater "independence," reduced dependence on the American relation, and the elimination of "inequalities." We can also expect Japan to increase pressure for resolving outstanding issues and to be much less tractable about air rights, fishery problems, tariff quotas, and other irritants that arise from time to time. Problems that we would consider simple bargaining issues, the Japanese are likely to see as matters of national honor, or as symbols of inequality of status. We can expect the Japanese to be more assertive in bargaining with us. Thumb-nosing gestures are likely to increase. While street demonstrations will continue to be a monopoly of the Left, strong language attacking the United States will not. The conservatives may find it necessary to compete with the Left in order to retain the support of an increasingly nationalistic public opinion.

Perennial problems such as Okinawa, American bases, and the Security Treaty are likely to peak somewhat earlier than had been expected. . . . Although much depends on the immediate atmosphere at the moment of negotiation, there is strong reason to believe that the Japanese would prefer to damp down mutual security arrangements to levels unacceptable to American policy, if not actually to scrap them in their present form. We would be wise to plan alternatives as soon as possible. . . .

Quite apart from military considerations, which must be left to experts, there are good political reasons to believe that we may lose more by remaining in Japan than by leaving it. Good will and friendly attitudes may not be easy to measure, but they are hard counters in the game of international relations. . . .

The most difficult single question, whatever the outcome of the Security Treaty negotiations, will be Okinawa. Once again it is the escalation in Vietnam that has pushed the timetable forward. In both Okinawa and Japan the fear of involvement through American bases will remain an important political factor exerting pressure on all sides. In order not to lose out in the competition with the socialists, the government may have to step up its own pace and press demands on the United States earlier than it had originally intended. The question we shall have to face well before the 1970s is whether Okinawa is worth holding from a political or even a military point of view. . . .

It is clear, then, that we are in for a good number of shocks. Disengagement is always painful, quite as much for the small changes it brings to our comfortable habits as for the big blows. . . .

First, we must learn to relax, to roll with the punches. There will be many things we do not like, but we should remember that most of them will probably not be fatal. . . .

Second, we must learn not only not to push, but to avoid the appearance of pushing. Japanese, as all close observers know, often assume that pressures are there even when they are not. They sometimes seem to anticipate pressures that have never been exerted, then act in response to their anticipations, and end up feeling that they have indeed been pressed. . . .

Third, we must be willing to let Japan do things on

her own and in her own way, even if we cannot approve of them at a particular time. There may be longer-range benefits that outweigh the immediate disadvantages. Japan's involvement with China and other communist countries, for example, may worry us. During the coming period, as long as the American-Chinese confrontation remains extreme, Japan may be expected at the very least to do things that we do not like, and at worst occasionally to support China against the United States. Certainly this will be worrisome. But in the long run, a Japan that is knowledgeable and realistic about Communist China is more valuable than one that is simultaneously fearful and romantic. . . .

Finally, what should be most obvious of all: we must not take Japan for granted. She is not automatically in our back pocket out of gratitude for our generosity after the war and the fine democratic reforms we brought her. Nor is she a benighted heathen, doing quite well of course, but still needing a guiding hand to lead her out of the wilderness. Japan is one of the great powers of the world. If we want her as ally or friend, we shall have to work at it.

The Meaning of Japanese History

Anyone who observes Japanese society with care will find countless ways in which the modern society maintains its ties with the past. Still, as we have seen, the Japanese have been so intent for the past century on catching up with the West that they sometimes appear almost anxious to cut the ties with their heritage. References in recent pages to a "spiritual vacuum" and the search for "unifying values" testify in some measure to this phenomenon.

An American scholar, speaking at a conference in Kyoto on the relation between Japanese and Western art, sees hints of the emergence of a new sense of historical identity while noting the reasons why it has taken so long to develop.

JOHN W. HALL

"Traditional Arts and the Japanese Sense of Historical Identity during a Hundred Years of Modern Change."

It is with a deep sense of nostalgia, . . . that I stand before you this morning. Kyoto is the city of my youth. I lived here in the days before the tower. I have known Hieizan in all its many moods, in fact I have climbed it on foot before the *doraivuwei* marred its flanks or the parking lot was carved out of the forest by the side of Komponchûdô. I should like to boast that I have known the "old" Kyoto. But each generation, it would seem, has observed the passing of this city's former glories, and KAMO-NO Chômei has preceded me in the lament for a better Kyoto. From Kamakura times to now, change is the essence of history. "The flow of the river is ceaseless and its water is never the same."

But if KAMO-NO Chômei was saddened by the decay of a Kyoto he once admired, what of us who have seen the transformation of the last hundred years? Has not the last century, which has brought Japan to its pinnacle of world prominence, been more ruinous to the old Kyoto than the entire eleven hundred years which preceded it? Is it not deeply significant that the emperor abandoned Kyoto in 1869 for Tokyo where he eventually took up his residence in a Western style palace? The currents of change in the last hundred years have placed Kyoto in double jeopardy. For the country of which it was once the capital has been swept by both the modernizing currents of technological change, and by powerful winds of influence from an alien civilization. The last hundred years have been hard on Kyoto and what it once stood for. And as a Sôseki or a TANIZAKI have expressed so eloquently in their works, this has been the source of deep disturbance for the artist and the writer in Japan. The question which they seem to ask is in our hearts as well. Can Kyoto be saved, and with it the cultural values that it once stood for? But should Kyoto be saved?

There are many in Japan who pay this city the supreme slight of profound indifference, and the guiding spirit of Kyoto itself seems bent on atonement for having escaped untouched from the last war by a continuous act of self-destruction.

A few years ago the American magazine *Show* had a feature issue on Japan under the title: "Japan, the New Far West." Frank Gibney, the editor, explained his view of Japan in these words:

> The theme words . . . Japan: the New Far West— suggest the reality and the excitement of an amazing and impressive, if at times gloriously confused, national culture. For despite its millennial tradition, Japan is a new country—new in its achievements, new in its brilliant economic pace and direction, new in the changes and widenings of its society. Despite its geographical location in what pre-jet generations used to call the Far East, Japan is a Western country.

This is, I suspect, a characteristically American (or should we say P.R.) view of Japan. But Gibney is certainly correct in suggesting the thrust of Japanese life today. And surely it is the quest for what is latest that creates the "glorious confusion" which so fascinates and disturbs the visitor to this country; which puts the television antenna on the thatched roof, or the refrigerator in the *tokonoma*, and gives birth to "flower arrangements" constructed of wire and colored plastic.

What is to become of Kyoto beyond this the hundredth year since the Restoration—this city which increasingly illustrates the visual and functional confusion between a Japanese way, which it carries off so superbly, and an international way, which it wears so awkwardly? Kyoto more than Tokyo forces upon us an awareness of the conflicts and tensions which still can be found in Japanese life, posing constantly the question of where Japan's historical past fits into its modern present. What is Kyoto to modern Japan? Has it not become a relic, simply a pre-"Meiji *mura*" on a gigantic scale? Is not Kyoto ultimately doomed, like so much of traditional life, to be bypassed or to succumb to the glacial advance of a homogeneous international style? Is it not destined in the end to be raised inert and detached like a Nubian monument above the rising waters of "progress."

Not that there is anything fundamentally wrong with inert preservation as such. It is admittedly a necessary first step. And the Japanese nation should be extremely gratified by the remarkable efforts which have been made to preserve its historic monuments, its art forms, and its craft techniques. Museums whether filled with objects or living persons (such as Imbe-yaki potters or Bunraku puppeteers) are essential to the survival of traditions. What is at issue, rather, is how traditions can inform the present? How they can continue as living forces in the present.

The fact is, of course, that we have in our midst, among the participants in this conference, men who begun to exemplify in their own creative works the answer to this question. And it is remarkable how similarly these men arrived at their powers of conscious interplay between Japanese tradition and the wider world audience. In none of the works of architecture, literature, drama, or music which we have admired was the simple act of preservation or imitation sufficient. Something else was required and that is the creative use through remembrance, or more often rediscovery, of meaning in a traditional form or mode. Moreover this creative act has been preceded by a sense of self-confidence which transcended both the act of mastery of a new and universal technique and the return to some newly discovered meaning in a traditional genre. It is dependent in other words on a degree of self-discovery, or, what I would like to call, a sense of historical identity.

This special quality which I refer to is required not simply by the artist but at large within the entire society.

And it is the quality which Kyoto must have if it is to remain alive in the years ahead. One would expect that within the society as a whole it would be the intellectual leaders, particularly the historians, who would articulate for the nation a philosophy of history adequate to modern demands. The fact that this has not been the case has contributed, I suspect, to a confusion of national mind which persists today, particularly in the academic, as against the business or professional, worlds.

Nations like individuals face the problem of finding meaning in their existence, of gaining self-knowledge about their sources of power and weakness, and about where they stand in history or among the nations of the world. The task is especially complicated for countries which are deeply involved in the process of modernization and nation-building, as in the United States, and even more when the process, as in the case of Japan, is so closely interwoven with foreign influence. Certainly for the Japanese nation, as for the individual, the last hundred years have made particularly difficult the acquisition of a secure sense of historical identity, a satisfying view of the historical process and of the relevance of Japan's past culture to it. It is no accident, in fact, that a major controversy exists in this country on how the last hundred years should be viewed and on how and why the Meiji centennial should be celebrated.

It is significant, I think, that Japan's entrance upon the course of rapid modernization came at a time of deep intellectual uncertainty within Japanese society itself. By the 1830's and 40's, few of the certainties which had comforted the eighteenth century Japanese were available to the Japanese intellectual. The Tokugawa shogunate no longer held the confidence of the nation. The fundamental efficacy of Buddhism and Confucianism was being questioned. China, which had so long stood as Japan's ultimate model, was losing its prestige. Social and political institutions which had stood for two centuries were proving inadequate. Unlike China, Japan faced the West, not at a time of supreme self-confidence but rather of self-questioning. And this had, I believe, implications both positive and negative. Positive in that there was no stubborn adherence to a rigid orthodoxy. Negative in that the search for self-assurance was greatly exacerbated.

After the middle of the nineteenth century, as we know, the West broke in upon Japan with irresistible prestige and with the claim to be master of the forces of progress. For several decades the current of change flowed all in one direction. Yet from the beginning the problem of historical identity was squarely faced. Could one become modern and yet somehow remain Japanese? Could one be Japanese without a basic denial of what was modern? The rethinking of Japan's traditional values began with such questions.

At this point, I suspect the Japanese faced problems of considerably greater magnitude and complexity than those encountered by Western societies at a comparable position in their development. The peoples of Europe could conceive of themselves as part of a great continuous stream of culture which emanated out of Greece, was enriched by Rome, diversified by tribal infiltrations, unified by the Christian Church, and finally activated by the wonders of science and industrial technology. The modern world was of their making; they admitted paternity for it, and could claim to know how it would grow up. Thus, we of the West, whether members of the greatest or the smallest nation, could feel ourselves part of the wave of the world's future. Our past was the past of this stream. The values we hold as essential to progress came out of our past. The political aspirations we hold for the future were first voiced by a Locke or a Rousseau or a Marx, in other words by our own intellectual forefathers.

None of these propositions held for the nineteenth century Japanese. They did not have a history which drew them out of the past and projected them into the future with the assurance that their forefathers had created the elements upon which the modern world was being built. They had no assurance that an inquiry into their early philosophers or historians would be significant or relevant to the problems of the present and the future. For many, in fact, history had become something from which to escape: the repository of those "base customs of former times" as the Five Clause Oath of 1868 put it, which had to be purged. For many the modern age started with a sort of historical self-rejection.

In his intellectual quest for historical identity in the modern world the Japanese historical philosopher was to pursue three possibilities leading to three types of individual and national response, and based upon three differing historical premises. First, one could remain a cultural traditionalist, a man who figuratively clung to his kimono in daytime and who shut himself up in a stubborn belief in Japan's unique cultural essence. For such a person, Japan's history was its own justification. Second, one could remain a religious traditionalist, holding to Buddhist and Confucian beliefs and to the existence of an all-Asian spiritual community. For such a person Asia was the center of world history. Finally, one could join the all-out effort to identify with the West and go modern. In this case, the West became the main, the normative, stream of world history.

No one of these responses was completely unreasonable, yet neither was any one of them to prove adequate in isolation. Each one, particularly when taken to extremes, has led to difficulties either for individual Japanese or for the nation. Nationalism based on belief in Japan's unlimited capacity provided the Japanese with the courage to strike out against the Western powers, yet it nurtured a cultural dogmatism and an exaggerated sense of national self-sufficiency and destiny which, as we know, was to be its own undoing. The patriotic histories of the 1940's are now but a relic of the war and are dismissed as propaganda.

The quest for an all-Asian spiritual unity was not irrational so much as it was unrealistic. OKAKURA, the popularizer of Japan's spiritual resistance to the West had claimed "Asia is one," united in its respect for religious values as against the coarse materialism of the West. Yet there had never been a unified Asia. And the all-Asia concept never served Japan particularly well, I suspect because most modern Japanese simply could not bring themselves to believe that their destinies were tied to the rest of Asia or that they should look to Asia rather than the West for leadership, or companionship, or emulation. As an integrating historical concept "Asia" has not been useful.

So it has been in the third category that the main Japanese effort to come to grips with modern requirements has been taken, and also in which the greatest uncertainties have lain. Ever since the arrival of Perry forced the issue of seclusion into the open the thinking Japanese has been confronted with the need to understand the West and to know how he and his society related to the stream of history which emanated from the West. Neither problem had ready answers. Certainly the Japanese did not have to transform themselves into Europeans, yet what was required of them? Was the essence of Western civilization Christianity? Was it simply its technology or science? Was it to be found in its arts and philosophies, or in terms of military might and national power? Meiji intellectual leaders struggled with these points. These questions led to more philosophical ones. What was the essential meaning of modern history? Was it simply a story of economic development originating in Europe? And hence was Japan simply another of the underdeveloped countries racing to catch up to those which had moved out ahead? Or was there some nobler scheme behind it all? Was the essential goal the nurturing of the free man and the creation of political democracy, or was it to be found in the achievement of a socialist Utopia? These are questions still being debated by many of my Japanese colleagues as they confront the issue of the Meiji centennial and its meaning.

I am afraid we in the West have not been of much aid to the Japanese in clarifying their historic status. Our historians and philosophers, until very recently at least, were content to write as though the only mankind worth knowing was their own. The world to them was simply the Western world, which having passed through stages of a classicism, feudalism, Renaissance, and early nationalism, had reached the ultimate achievement of the democratic national state. Where did Japan belong in such a scheme? Did Japan have a classical age, or a Renaissance? (The Kyoto historian NISHIDA Naojirô wrote a brilliant cultural history which worked with such ideas, but his work has long been forgotten.) And what in Japan's past could nourish ideas of freedom, individualism, and democracy? (The attempt to find an anti-feudal political writer in Tokugawa times has turned up only a maverick ANDÔ Shôeki.) Rather, had not Japan's past been the antitheses of these qualities? And so, if Japan was to join the modern world, must not it renounce its past and start over? Many recent historians in Japan have written as though they were ashamed of their own history; the denial of 1868 as a worthy national symbol reflects this same attitude.

As individuals and as a nation the Japanese have needed a philosophy of history which could offer their past a place in the modern present, not simply as an exotic memory or as a millstone around the national neck. They have needed a view of history which could accept modern Japan not simply as a curious misfit among the Western societies, but as a legitimate member of the in group—a people who had achieved the modern condition through a normal sequence of growth out of their own past rather than as a gift, a benefice, from the West. And it is perhaps for this reason that Japanese writers have been so attracted to *systems* of history, that Marxism or Weberianism have had such an appeal. For these systems which purport universal applicability offer Japanese history a place in the struggle of all mankind for his own betterment. Yet the trouble with the universal models heretofore available has been that they too have arisen out of Western experience and that they have generally been applied normatively. They have for this reason tended to cast Japanese history into an unfavorable light, as forever inadequately trying to catch up. Meiji becomes an unworthy symbol because it did not achieve enough, enough that is when measured against an abstract norm derived from Europe.

The solution to Japan's problem of historical relevance hinges on the capacity of the Japanese to believe that their country is capable of becoming modern without losing its national or cultural identity, to believe, in other words, that the Japanese past can hold lessons for the present. Yet where is this conviction to come from when the nation's historians remain unconvinced, remain unconvinced even after the Japanese people themselves in their postwar reincarnation have become in so many ways living proof of this proposition? I submit that the answer is beginning to appear right here among the men represented at this conference, the artists, dramatists, novelists, architects, these men who have created modern works of art which are yet distinctly Japanese have done more than the uncertain theorist. For each one of their works draws into the modern stream of Japanese life a piece of the Japanese past It does more; it leads into the stream of modern world history a new tributary from out of Japanese culture. (I must say I am particularly impressed by the example of the Kyoto International Conference Hall—in its use of materials, themes, and settings.)

The consequences of all of this are enormous, not only for the psychological implications they hold for the Japanese people, but for the field of historical interpretation in Japan, and beyond Japan for the entire world.

First off, it permits rehabilitation of Japanese history as something important in and of itself. This is not a return to Japanese history from a nationalistic point of view. It is the antithesis of such, for it proceeds from a world view which looks out upon the world, not compartmented by nations or separate areas—much less divided into East and West—but unified and hence, uniformly subject to the historian's basic theories about human development. Japanese history, thus, is part of world history.

I suspect the problem heretofore was to some extent complicated by the heavy emphasis on the political and social aspects of national development, in which fields the West admittedly has produced the most articulate philosophers and theorists. But even in these aspects of modern life, as the emphasis shifts from philosophies of action to those of adjustment, the Japanese and the world will find more and more that is worthy of study in the Japanese past. The field of art is informative. For it reveals graphically how the question of historical identity can be solved. As we have seen, it is not enough simply that a style of painting or a way of acting is perpetuated unchanged. There is a matter of transformation or assimilation, either by translation into modern idiom or by rediscovery from a modern point of view. This is precisely what we have seen happen in each of the art forms discussed at this meeting. In each there has been a cycle, first of rejection or neglect of the past, then of rediscovery (often under foreign impetus), then of preservation, and finally of assimilation and recreation into something new. The old techniques, as such, may not be fully mastered, the old aesthetic principles may even be misunderstood, but something new is created through a rediscovery of something of importance in the past. (The "discovery" of the Japanese musical tradition that Professor Borris writes of required the efforts of both Japanese and Western musicians.) The past can nourish the present only through such rediscovery by those who themselves are fundamentally comfortable in the present. And this applies to the development of historical interpretation as well. Discovery of relevancies, of lessons, in the past, not just failures to match a supposed ideal pattern can perhaps come only when the Japanese intellectual comes to believe that the race is over, that Japan's present and future problems are not so different from those faced by America and the countries of Europe. Only then can the Japanese historian be induced to look to his past for models which may yet prove more adequate to the needs of the individual in a modern world in which the political objectives of a Locke or a Marx have both become inadequate.

And so I return to the question of Kyoto and its preservation. The key is rediscovery. It is not sufficient simply that we can go to Ryôanji* and sit, and marvel, without knowing why. We must unlock the mystery of the genius of that work of art in terms that hold meaning for us today. Kyoto is doomed to Museum-like existence as long as it is content to stand at its entrances and fatten itself off the fees it collects from its tourist visitors. Ryôanji has already been desecrated in the name of tourism. If as we are told space and time are the essence of Japanese architecture, then what is left of the essence of Ryôanji when we are driven by car to within a step of its main building, are given one or two minutes to absorb the garden and then are hustled away to make room for another rush of tourists? But there are other unspoiled spots, I was told some years ago. There is Entsûji the "thinking man's Ryôanji." But Entsûji has now been discovered by the tourist. Where do we go now? The prospect of continual flight before the onrush of the Kankô [tourist] bus is frightening. No—flight is not the answer. Kyoto must stand its ground and defend itself. But to do

---

* A famous landscape garden.

this Kyoto must know itself sufficiently so that it can protect its essence rather than its exterior—its spirit not just its monuments. Moreover it must know what that essence is and it must be able to prove to its own people and to the world that it is not simply age that makes monuments worth viewing, rather that these monuments are repositories of certain living values which are needed in the modern world.

BIBLIOGRAPHY OF SELECTIONS

AIKAWA, T. *Unwilling Patriot*. Tokyo: Jordan Press, 1960.

DRUCKER, PETER. "Japan Tries for a Second Miracle." *Harper's*, March 1963.

Facts About Japan, no. 81. New York: Consulate General of Japan, 1963.

FAIRBANK, J. K., REISCHAUER, EDWIN O., and CRAIG, A. M. *East Asia: The Modern Transformation*. Boston: Houghton Mifflin, 1964.

HACHIYA, MICHIHIKO. *Hiroshima Diary*. Chapel Hill: University of North Carolina Press, 1955.

HALL, JOHN W. "Traditional Arts and the Japanese Sense of Historical Identity During a Hundred Years of Modern Change." Lecture delivered on September 30, 1968 at the meeting of "International Round Table on the Relation between Japanese and Western Arts."

HALL, JOHN W., BEARDSLEY, R. K. *Twelve Doors to Japan*. New York: McGraw-Hill, 1965.

ITO, HIROBUMI. *Commentaries on the Constitution of the Empire of Japan*. Trans. Ito Myoji. Tokyo, 1889.

The Japan Year Book 1939–1940. Tokyo, 1939. (Also in Tiedemann. *Modern Japan*. Princeton, N.J.: Van Nostrand, 1957.)

KEENE, DONALD. *Japanese Literature: An Introduction for Western Readers*. London: John Murray.

———. *Living Japan*. New York: Doubleday, 1959.

———, ed. *Anthology of Japanese Literature*. New York: Grove Press, 1955.

———, ed. *Modern Japanese Literature: An Anthology*. New York: Grove Press, 1960.

KIDDER, J. E. *Ancient Japan*. London: Weidenfeld and Nicolson, 1965. New York: The John Day Co.

KOSAKA, MASATAKA. "A Japanese View of America." *Harper's*, May 1965.

McLaren, W. W., ed. "Japanese Government Documents." *Transactions of the Asiatic Society of Japan* (Tokyo) 42 (1914).

Morris, Ivan. *The World of the Shining Prince.* New York: Knopf, 1964.

Nihong: Chronicles of Japan from the Earliest Times to A.D. 670. Trans. W. G. Aston. London: Allen & Unwin, 1956.

Nitobe, Inazo. *Bushido: The Soul of Japan.* New York: Putnam, 1905.

Passin, Herbert, ed. *The United States and Japan.* Englewood Cliffs, N.J.: Prentice-Hall, 1966.

Reischauer, Edwin O. *Beyond Vietnam.* New York: Knopf, 1967.

————. *The United States and Japan.* Cambridge, Mass.: Harvard University Press, 1957.

Reischauer, Edwin O., and Fairbank, J. K. *East Asia: The Great Tradition.* Boston: Houghton Mifflin, 1958.

Shukan Bunshun. As trans. and summarized in *The Japan Times,* January 3, 1969 under the title "The Season of Instant Worshippers."

Ryu, Shintaro. "Resetting the Course." *Japan Quarterly* 12 (January 1965).

Storry, R. *A History of Modern Japan.* Baltimore: Penguin Books, 1960.

Tsunoda, Ryusaku, DeBary, W. T., and Keene, Donald, eds. *Sources of Japanese Tradition.* New York: Columbia University Press, 1964.

Warner, Langdon. *The Enduring Art of Japan.* New York: Grove Press, 1959. (Originally published Cambridge, Mass.: Harvard University Press, 1952.)

GLOSSARY

Pronunciation guide: Consonants are read as in English (with "g" always hard)

        Vowels:

           a   as in "ah" or "depart"
           i   as in "machine"
           u   as in "rule"
           e   as in "end"
           o   as in "note"

AWARE　A favortite term in classical (10th-11th centuries) Japanese literature. May suggest "pathetic," "moving," "beautiful." Often used in the phrase MONO NO AWARE which suggests the inseparability of beauty and sadness.

BUSHI　A warrior, a knight.

BUSHIDO　"The way of the warrior," the code of the perfect warrior.

DAIMYO　A feudal lord.

DORAIVUWEI　Driveway, toll road. An example of the thousands of English and other foreign terms which have been incorporated in the Japanese language in modern times.

GENRO　An elder. The term is commonly used to denote the top leaders of the Meiji era after they had retired but still exerted great influence in political affairs.

GETA　Wooden clogs.

GONINGUMI　"Five-man groups." Neighborhood groups organized by the Tokugawa government to aid in controlling the lives of the commonfolk.

GOSHINEI　Portraits of the Emperor and Empress. The portraits were accorded semi-sacred treatment in Japanese schools between 1890 and 1945.

HAN　A feudal domain.

HARAKIRI　Suicide by disembowelment.

HINOKI　Japanese cypress.

HOANJO　A room accomodating the Imperial Portraits.

KAKEMONO   A vertical scroll; either a painting or calligraphy or both. Usually hung in a TOKONOMA (see below).

KAMME   A measure of weight (no longer in use).

KAMI   A spirit, the dieties of the Shinto religion.

KAMIDANA   A shelf for Shinto paraphernalia; still found in many homes.

KANKO   Tourism, sightseeing.

KARMA   The Hindu concept, absorbed by Buddhism, which asserts that deeds committed in one lifetime will have moral consequences for the next.

KASUTERA   A sponge cake, originally introduced to Japan by the Portuguese in the 16th century.

KIMONO   An ankle-length, wide-sleeved robe peculiar to Japan. Today women often wear silk kimonos at formal occasions, while both sexes may wear cotton kimonos when relaxing at home.

KOJIKI   One of two histories of Japan written in the 8th century. Both works, written in Chinese and much influenced by official Chinese dynastic histories, contain both myth and fact.

KOTATSU   A heating device consisting of a low table covered by a quilt. The charcoal brazier which traditionally provided heat has been displaced by an electric heater.

KYOIKU CHOKUGO   The Imperial Rescript on Education issued in 1890. A key step in the effort to foster Emperor-centered nationalism in modern Japan. A dead letter since 1945.

MEIJI MURA   A "village" established in the late 1960's in which artifacts of the Meiji period are being assembled and displayed.

NICHIREN   The name of a major Buddhist sect and of its founder-priest. Founded in 1253, it is the only major Buddhist sect native to Japan. Several so-called 'new religions' have their roots in Nichiren Buddhism (see SOKA GAKKAI).

NIHON (NIPPON)   Japan.

NIHONGI   One of the two original histories of Japan (see KOJIKI).

RANGAKU   "Dutch studies." (Books from Holland were the only materials from the West available in Japan during the Tokugawa period.)

SAMURAI   Warrior or knight (see BUSHI).

SANKIN KOTAE   The Tokugawa policy requiring DAIMYO to reside in Edo (Tokyo) every other year. One of many devices used to prevent DAIMYO from threatening the status quo.

SHINTO   A religion native to Japan.

SHISHI Samurai dedicated to the overthrow of the Tokugawa during the twenty years prior to the Meiji Restoration (1868). These men were responsible for many political murders and other acts of violence.

SOHYO The General Council of Japanese Labor Unions. A labor federation which has been the main pillar of support for the Japan Socialist Party.

SOKA GAKKAI A so-called "new religion" which has experienced phenomenal growth in membership since 1950.

TANUKI Badger.

TATAMI A floor-covering composed of tightly woven rice-straw three inches thick with a woven reed mat stitched on top. These 6' by 4' 'mats' provide the standard measurement for the multi-use rooms of the Japanese house.

TOFU Soy bean curd.

TOKONOMA An alcove used to display vertical scrolls, flower arrangements, and other works of art.

TONARIGUMI "Neighborhood group." A modern version of the GONINGUMI described above. Abolished in 1945.

UJI The lineage groups ("clans") of elite families during the Yamato period. A number of kin-related families under a single main family comprised a single UJI.

YOKI "Good." A term used in classical literature denoting good lineage and (therefore) proper appreciation of beauty.

ZAIBATSU The five or six huge business combines which dominated Japan's industrial economy until 1945. All remain powerful today though anti-monopoly laws have forced widened ownership and looser ties between the myriad companies of a single group.

ZEN A Buddhist sect which originated in India, passed on to China, but had its greatest impact in feudal Japan.

INDEX